LIVING POETRY

ENGLISH POETRY FROM KERALA
Seven Contemporary Poets

Kamala Das
Anna Sujatha Mathai
Meena Alexander
Gopikrishnan Kottoor
C P Surendran
Jeet Thayil
Vijay Nambisan

Chosen & Edited by Gopikrishnan Kottoor
Foreword by K Satchidanandan

KAVYA-ADISAKRIT

TITLE: **LIVING POETRY: ENGLISH POETRY FROM KERALA, SEVEN CONTEMPORARY POETS**

Authors: Kamala Das, Anna Sujatha Mathai, Meena Alexander, Gopikrishnan Kottoor, C P Surendran, Jeet Thayil, Vijay Nambisan

Chosen & Edited by: Gopikrishnan Kottoor,

Designed and Published by: Adisakrit Publishing Services
Chennai-600119, India
www.adisakrit.com

Bound and Printed by Amazon

Edition 1, First Published: May 2021

ISBN: 9798503292619

Copyright © for each poem rests with its poet

Cover Photograph Copyright © Gopikrishnan Kottoor

All photographs provided by the poets as credited

All rights reserved.

No part of this book may be reproduced in any form or by any electronic or mechanical means including information storage and retrieval systems, without permission in writing from the author. The only exception is by a reviewer, who may quote short excerpts in a review.

ACKNOWLEDGEMENTS AND PERMISSIONS

Acknowledgements are made to the following imprints and copyright holders in respect of permissions to excerpt poems for this anthology.

Kamala Das
Collected Poems: Published by Penguin Random House India, 2014 Copyright © Jaisurya Das 2014. Poems published by arrangement with Penguin Random House India 2014.

Anna Sujatha Mathai
The Attic of Night: Published by Rupa and Co, Noida 1991. Copyright © Anna Sujatha Mathai 1991. Life on my Side of the Street: Published by Sahitya Akademi, New Delhi 2005. Copyright © Anna Sujatha Mathai 2005. Mother's Veena and Other Poems: Published by Authorspress New Delhi 2013.Copyright © Anna Sujatha Mathai 2013. Poems included by permission of the author.

Meena Alexander
Illiterate Heart Published by Triquarterly Books/Northwestern University Press, USA 2002. Copyright © Meena Alexander 2002. All rights reserved. Quickly Changing River: Published by Triquarterly Books/Northwestern University Press USA. 2008. Copyright © Meena Alexander 2008 All rights reserved. Birthplace with Buried Stones: Published by Triquarterly Books/Northwestern University Press USA 2013. Copyright © Meena Alexander 2013. All rights reserved.
Atmospheric Embroidery: Published by Hachette India Book Publishing, India Pvt Ltd 2015. Copyright © Meena Alexander 2015. Published by arrangement with Hachette Book Publishing, India Pvt. Ltd. Gurgaon. 122003- India.

Gopikrishnan Kottoor
The Painter of Evenings: Published by Poetrywala, Paperwall Media Pvt Ltd, Mumbai 2018. Copyright © Gopikrishnan Kottoor 2018. Poems published by permission of the author.

C P Surendran
Available Light: Published by Speaking Tiger Publishing Private Limited, New Delhi 2017. Copyright© CP Surendran 2017. Poems published by

arrangement with Speaking Tiger Publishing Private Limited, New Delhi and by permission of the author.

Jeet Thayil
Collected Poems: Published by Aleph Book Company, New Delhi 2015. Copyright© Jeet Thayil 2015. Poems published with permission of the author and in arrangement with Aleph Book Company, New Delhi.

Vijay Nambisan
These Were My Homes: Published by Speaking Tiger Publishing Private Limited, 2019. Copyright © Vijay Nambisan Trust 2019 and Kavery Nambisan. Poems published by permission of Vijay Nambisan Trust, Kavery Nambisan, and in arrangement with Speaking Tiger Publishing Private Limited, New Delhi.

Geetha Nair G, formerly Associate Professor of English, All Saints College, Trivandrum, Kerala, for editorial assistance and additional introductory inputs.

Dedication
Vishnu Narayanan Namboothiri
(1939-2021)

'You have to understand, when I saw her (Meena Alexander) use the word Kerala in a poem (long after I finished grad school) I wept....'

Poet Aimee Nezhukumatathil,
Pushcart Prize Winner,
Professor, MFA Program,
University of Mississippi, USA.

TABLE OF CONTENTS

Acknowledgements and Permissions iii
Foreword 13
Introduction 15

KAMALA DAS 33

March of the Mercenaries 35
The Magnolia 36
The Sensuous Woman 37
Scalpels 38
I Dare Not Gaze Again 38
The Maples Are Green Still 39
A Feminist's Lament 40
Larger than Life Was He 41
Too Late for Making up 42
The Maggots 43
The Anamalai Poems 44

ANNA SUJATHA MATHAI 49

Perfume 51
Out of Reach 52
Coming Running Jumping 53
My Lost Language 54
Ishvari's Voice 55
Stones 56
On the Beach at Baga 57
Song of the Fall 58
In Tiruvella 59

Light	62
Frozen	63
Goddess Without Arms	63
Mother's Stories	64
Time and the Woman	65
The Woman Before	66
You're Mine, Not Death's	67
The Woman in the Falling House	69
Hysteria	70
At Least Songs	72
Death and the Poet	73

MEENA ALEXANDER *75*

Muse	77
She Speaks: A School Teacher from South India	78
Dog Days of Summer	80
Cadenza	81
Lychees	81
For My Father, Karachi 1947	82
Hyderabad Notebook	83
Bright Passage	86
Moksha	87
No Rescue (with Toy Cars)	88
Sarra Copia accused of Heresy in the year 1641	89
Univocity	90
Provincetown by the Sea	90
Scrim-Scram of Music	91
Torn Branches	92
Ars Poetica	93
Lines with Red Ants	93
Bathtub Blues	94
This is not a Dream	94

Black Sand at the Edge of the Sea 95
Debt Ridden 95
Aesthetic knowledge 96
Udisthanam 97

GOPIKRISHNAN KOTTOOR 99

Flamingos, Vashi Creek, New Mumbai 101
Mother's Sarees 101
Vagator Beach, Goa 103
Mumbai Blasts 104
From 'Father, Wake us in Passing' 105
    i.   America 105
    ii.   Telephone Call 105
    iii. Prison House 106
    iv. Nectar of the Gods 106
    v.   Lone Ranger 107
    vi. Gift 107
    vii. ICU 108
    viii. The Colours of Pain 109
    ix. Angels on the Moon 109
    x.   Sea Crabs 110
    xi. Wedding Night 110
Visiting the Institute of English, 40 Years Later. 111
Nudes on the Beach 113
The Painter of Evenings 113
Digging 114
Dash* 115

C. P. SURENDRAN 117

A Note to the Self from Tranquebar 119
Options for an Old Man in a Far Room 120
House Hunting 122

Back 123
Signature 123
Two 124
Reflection 125
Sparrows 125
Harbinger 126
Prospect 127
From Catafalque 128
Post Natal 128
Threshold 129
Rout 130
Permanent Revolution 130
I 131
Post Crypt 132
Homage to a Hen 132
Dog 133
Boy 133
Translation 134

JEET THAYIL *135*

Self-Portrait 137
Future Watercolour 137
Separation's Sonnet 138
Boyhood 138
53 Views of Abstraction, 1 Rhyme, 0 Blackbirds 139
The Heroin Sestina 141
Trout Fishing at Night 142
Fixing Father 143
Pushkin Knew Heaven 143
Apocalypso 144
Imaginary Homecoming 145

Yet Another Mother Poem	147
For Agha Shahid Ali	148
New Year, Goa	149
Malayalam's Ghazal	149
Letter from a Mughal Emperor, 2006	150
My Lie	153
Where This One Came From	153
My Grandmother's Funeral	155
Wedding Picture	156

VIJAY NAMBISAN 157

The Miracle of the Pomegranate	159
Madras Central	159
Cats Have No Language	160
The Attic	161
Grandfather's Beard	162
Poetic Licence	163
After Six Drinks	164
Holy, Holy	164
Narcissus in the Drought	165
Ducks	166
Snow	167
The Door	168
These Were My Homes	169
Integument	169
My Father's Hand	170
My Mother Would Not	171
Double Bill	171
L' après -midi d'un Canard	172
Familial: One Gift My Father Gave Me	172
The Rain is Pouring down Again	173

Gopikrishnan Kottoor 175

FOREWORD

'*Living Poetry: English Poetry from Kerala, Seven Contemporary Poets*' is perhaps the first attempt to bring together some of the more important poetic voices from Kerala writing in English in a single volume. There are at least a dozen more Malayali poets I know who write well in English but whose oeuvre is probably not large enough to be represented in such a collection. The significance of this attempt is best summed up in the subtitle of the book with its double accent: English and Kerala, for, these poets, most of whom spent a considerable part of their life outside Kerala, or even India, bring into their poetry a lot of their regional memories and associations thus enriching the bi-lingual sensibility that underlies a lot of Indian poetry written in English, poets like Arun Kolatkar, Dilip Chitre or Gopal Honnalgere being some outstanding examples. It was Ayyappa Paniker, poet and scholar and the editor of one of the earliest anthologies of Indian poetry in English who had first pointed to the existence of regional and mother-tongue influences in poetry subsumed under the umbrella-term 'Indian English poetry' and remarked that many of the poets known thus belonged as much to their regions and languages as to the nation. He even spoke of using terms like Marathi English, Gujarati English, Malayali English, etc as the sensibilities of these poets are inflected, if not altogether moulded, by their regions, in cultural as well as linguistic terms.

    This anthology is an important and necessary intervention in the field especially in times when our cultural diversity is under threat from forces of standardization.

K. SATCHIDANANDAN

INTRODUCTION

Kerala is any writer's dream land. Arundhati Roy proved it in her epoch making novel, "The God of Small Things". Now well known to the rest of the world as God's own country for its natural beauty, even one who is not a poet cannot escape the lasting allure that Kerala casts on his psyche. Kerala has an endoscopic culture all its own, well amalgamated with temples, churches, mosques, and is deeply rooted in myth, cymballed ceremonies, and tradition. The essential poetic psyche of the Kerala poet writing poetry in English springs from this ambivalence.

For most Kerala poets writing in English, the Tharavad or Ancestral House with its kinship in the larger joint family system, and its 'ghosts' of ancestral dominance emerge as a cardinal or recurring theme. In many of the poems of Kamala Das the Nalappattu Tharavad becomes larger than life and is intrinsic to her poetic core.

> *There is a house now far away where once*
> *I received love.... That woman died,*
> *The house receded into silence.*
>
> ("My Grandmother's House")

A childhood that is kaleidoscopic in the subconscious, follows him or her everywhere. Traditions, customs, and conventions illumined in nostalgia emerge as major themes linking the poet and his or her life-work. A commonality engaging the cultural identity thus marks most of the Kerala English poets. Unlike perhaps, in many other cultures even within India, the larger joint family within its matriarchal system has always been compelling, pervading the poet's sensitive soul. As Kamala Das continues,

> *How often I think of going*
> *There, to peer through blind eyes of windows or*
> *Just listen to the frozen air...*

It is clearly difficult for the Kerala poet to break away from his or her past bearings. The dark roots of ancestry soaked in home longings are densely fibrous in memory content. The theme also surfaces vividly in the poems of Vijay Nambisan such as "The Attic" or "Grandfather's Beard".

The lie of the water-logged land is a subconscious precipitate as when Jeet Thayil writes

> *As a boat in Muvattupuzha about to drop*
> *Its load of two children and a woman*
> *Into the monsoon current....*
>
> ("The Haunts" — Collected Poems)

Or when they spark memories as in the daintiness of childhood nostalgia of Meena Alexander's haunting mother-daughter poem

> *Childhood is a hot country, amma lives there.*
> *The sky has turned the colour of torn grass.*
> *Think of the calf dragged away to Changanasseri Fair*
> *Tiny tottering thing, snout wet with gooseberry juice.*
>
> ("Torn Grass" — Quickly Changing River)

Tiruvalla, the quaint village town in Kerala has to be Tiruvalla, even in Chicago or New York, or England, and a young Meena Alexander or Anna Sujatha are totally ensconced in those memories. The land of origin becomes both a catharsis and a release for the English language poet from Kerala. The yearning for the 'lost home' is forlorn as in Anna Sujatha

> *And the old house in Tiruvella*
> *is faded now.*
> *We too will fade and die, and our lives*
> *remain a mystery.*
>
> ("In Tiruvella")

The *wordscape* is Malayalam, and the *thoughtscape* is the growing up mind saturated with Kerala's palm fringed coast line, backwaters, rivers, rich blue lagoons, sea facing thatched huts and grassy hillscapes.

Equally distressing therefore for the poet is the thought of the native language disrobed from him or her, and the engagements and disengagements they create within, that seek wistful responses in their poetry. Thus the language of origin, Malayalam, still forms a dormant haven for a Kerala poet's expression in English, with the dormancy occasionally spilling over as we see in the poems of Meena Alexander or Anna Sujatha Mathai. In a poem such as 'Muse', Malayalam words that are closest to relationships or childhood entities such as *penne* (girl) *pustakam* (book) must appear in the English poem to free the poet and to allow for a spontaneous, poetic flow. In the poem "Attic" by Vijay Nambisan the refrain of the word Unni, (little one) alerts us to the poet's compulsive need to use the Malayalam term for which no replacement in any other language would suffice. Anna Sujatha must use the endearing term *mole* (daughter), *inja*, (traditional scrubber) *kashava kauni* (gold bordered female clothing) or *mundu* (dothi) thus injecting in her verse 'Keralasqueness', satisfactorily for herself, making up for the lost language.

We see an emotional let-down in the vacuum of not being at home in his home language in the poet Jeet Thayil. In his poem "Malayalam's Ghazal" Jeet has his father prompt him to show himself as a successful poet by writing a ghazal in Malayalam.

> *When you are too long in rooms of English,*
> *Open your window to the fresh air of Malayalam.*
> ....
> *I greet you, my ancestors, O scholars and linguists.*
> *My father who recites Baudelaire in Malayalam.*
>
> *Jeet, such drama with the scraps you know.*
> *Write a couplet, if you dare, in Malayalam.*

Of all the poets included in this anthology, perhaps it could be that Jeet alone is closest to thinking spontaneously in English as he writes his poems. As he says in his poem "English"

> *...and I would be ruined still by syntax, the risk*
> *And worry of committing word to stone*
> *English fills my right hand, silence the left.*

For most part, such filling and silence could be on account of alienation from one's own language from an early age that is not without a tinge of guilt. Thus perhaps in Jeet's poems, (and only in the peripheral sense), the notion of inner belonging of the Kerala kind is much more narrow as thematically he is more pan-Indian just perhaps as Tishani Doshi is, where her use of the Gujarati birth element is not stronger than her use of her current south Indian background to suit her poetry. In Vijay Nambisan, the break down on account of the language barrier and his inability to write in it, is a regretful lament as expounded in his introduction to his translations of Poontanam and Melpattur. In Kamala Das, the ability to write in both Malayalam and English,

> *I speak three languages,*
> *write in two, dream in one'*

("An Introduction")

provides her with a winning edge. We see that in Kamala Das, who is largely self-taught, and for most part autobiographical, her poems have the imagery and flavour that is intensely of the Malayalam kind.

> *the silence of old trees*
> *adorning your family home*
> *which remember you as a child*

("Scalpels")

In Anna Sujatha Mathai, the need to retrieve the loss of a lost tongue is like the yearning for the return of the lost lover

> *My lost language Malayalam,*
> *Has dropped like a gold wedding band,*
> *Which slipped off the finger*
> *Into the stream below,*
> *A lost bond lying*
> *In the flowing water....*

("My Lost Language")

Anna Sujatha gainfully captures most of the lost shades of love, lineage, language, ancestry and home. Just like Meena Alexander or Vijay,

> *My lost language shines in the palm of my hand.*
> *...........*
> *A language that trembles in my deepest sleep.*

In her fine moments Anna Sujatha can reach the zenith of poetry's incandescence.

> *We are all called to the same Festival,*
> *And are but fragments*
> *Falling, bright sparks from a careless hand—*
> *Children, for a brief day in the sunlight*
> *Before the dark waters embrace us.*

("Death and the Poet")

In several of the Malayali women poets writing in English, themes such as the shackles of patriarchy, the bonds that cripple Indian women and looking for ways to break free, occur. These traits are seen both in Kamala Das and Sujatha Mathai.

The colour of the skin could be an underlying obsession with many poets especially the women poets such as Kamala Das

> *very brown,*
> *born in Malabar,*

("An Introduction")

Or where Meena Alexander who called herself "a woman cracked by multiple migrations" writes often of her favourite colour "Indigo" that appears almost as an euphemism for the colour of her Indian skin and as she reveals in "Indigo"

> *O muse of my migrancy*
> *black rose*
> *of the southern shore*
> *...*
> *I search for myself*

in the map of indigo.

and in her revealing lament

> *I am a poet writing in America. But American poet? An Asian America poet then?... A woman poet; of colour, a South-Indian who makes up lines in English... A third world woman poet.*

("Fault Lines"—A Memoir)

Closer home, the kind of boldness and the leads Kamala brought to Indian women poets writing in English were abrasive and revolutionary.

> *Impotent male who with a grin,*
> *Of pride calls himself a sadist.....*

And again,

> *You could not ejaculate but*
> *I ignored the flaw.*

("The Magnolia")

Anna has recourse to a safer tread, as in "Light" when she concludes:

> *She who seeks light*
> *Must learn to walk in the darkness*
> *On her own road.*

("Light")

Kamala Das resorts to yielding only where sex is concerned, making her courage powerless as in "A Feminist's Lament".

> *What was courage worth at the very end?*
> *Even Phoolan the dacoit queen finally threw down her gun*
> *to settle for weekly orgasms.*

("A Feminist's Lament")

Theme wise, and thought pattern wise, the resemblances between Anna Sujatha and Kamala Das are numerous enough that one could even be a foil for the other, though Anna Sujatha is more comfortable in a conventional poetic attire.

For an eminent Malayalam poet as K Satchidanandan, a professor of English who is now being increasingly read as an English language poet in contemporary Indian English poetry anthologies with his own English translations of Malayalam poetry, there is no big divide. This presents a contrast to the distinguished English professor and celebrated Malayalam poet Ayyappa Paniker who consciously would not be part of the English language poetry scene, though he had his own translations of his Malayalam poems into English and was also a pioneering champion in promoting English language poetry in India.

The poems of Satchidanandan, like those of Kamala Das, Anna Sujatha or the early Meena Alexander, make it clear that, as with Ayyappa Paniker, their intrinsic poetic cultivation, especially in their embryonic forms render themselves primarily in the native medium before they have their outer expression in English.

Where much of the poet's childhood has been outside Kerala, the sense of belonging or origin is also partially lost and the native ethos is not so vibrantly visible. A case in point is perhaps seen in the poems of Aimee Nezhukumatathil, settled since childhood in the USA, whose father was a Keralite. With native moorings not too strong, the poetry also detaches itself from native character, as experienced in Aimee's poems where one cannot find the typical Malayali liquorice. However, the nostalgia, though distant, is still visible and the genetic code cannot be utterly broken as when Amiee reminisces in her remembrance lectures on Meena Alexander:

"Meena was the very first poet I discovered who named places and sounds and smells and sights from Kerala, the emerald green, southernmost coast of Kerala, a place I love so deeply in my veins and lungs but never saw in any poems brought into my classes or any book I could find in our suburban libraries. You have to understand that I made it through twenty years of schooling and no poet from India was ever brought into my classroom. You have to understand that I was once in a workshop where my cohort wanted me to italicize the word "mango" because it was too "exotic". You have to understand, when I saw her use the word Kerala in a poem (long after I finished grad school) I wept...."

Just as the lie of the land, nostalgia and ancestry are thematic markers for the general poetry in the making, so are relationships. It is particularly fascinating to observe how the father figure shapes or promotes poetical density especially with the poets included in this anthology. The father child communion is visibly stronger in the male poets but is a heart rending theme in the poems of Meena Alexander, just as in Sharon Olds, where the father- daughter relationship is strong, but here the keynote is also a ripped away memory of homeland, which is the soul spring of Meena's poetry

> *I hear my father's voice on the phone,*
> *He wants me to come from America to see him*
> *he does not want to die and be put in the earth*
> *my sweet father: who held me high above the water*
> *of the red sea when I was five...*

("Alexander, 2002")

The Father poems of the poets are often painfully retrospective, and separation from loved ones bring about some of their finest outpourings in verse as in Gopi Kottoor's "Father, Wake us in Passing",

> *But you said, son,*
> *I must sleep now.*
> *Then you turned over*
> *Late that night, dipping your head onto a pillow of stars,*
> *Your brain entangling the milk way,*
> *While I walked out into a misted Fall morning*
> *On the other side of the earth,*
> *The rain pouring entirely*
> *Out of my empty hands.*

("The Telephone Call")

Surendran's "Catafalque" poems on his father are a searing experience.

> *But put a collar on him, he said, a name*
> *And an address, so people know*
> *Where he comes from, where to go.*

Introduction

("Dog")

It is interesting to observe how the 'father' has the primary role in the future shaping of the poetry of Kottoor

> *I have now set out to do the things*
> *You loved most about me.*
> *About a gift called poetry.*

("Gift")

The fervor is the same with the poet Vijay Nambisan,

> *Another gift he gave, and that was love*
> *Of words. How they come together, make*
> *A song.*

("One Gift my Father Gave Me")

Here is CP Surendran acknowledging his father for his 'gift', on his death,

> *I am in debt to all I see and hear, paddy glittering*
> *Green in the field of day, the stream plucking its way*
> *Through stars, the moon caught in flight in a throng*
> *Of thorns. Your gifts are at work even after death.*

("Translation")

Gratitude to his father wells up as atonement in Jeet Thayil,

> *I beg now of you, father, I forgive*
> *The tireless eruptions of the flesh.*
> *Even in death I do your will.*

("Fixing Father")

Gopi Kottoor's poetic accomplishment lies in his ability to touch everyday objects with beauty, linking them to our lives. His poems, deft, understated, conjure landscapes where private agonies as well as sensual dreams become universal. Kottoor can also be down to earth, and for him

> *Mud-work is a kind of worship,*

A silent thanksgiving for a home called earth.

("Digging")

He can transform himself into a poet of love.

What you were to me,
And what you still are
I just cannot fathom
Just as no ocean
Fathoms its icebergs
All lit with borrowed stars.

("Are You There?" – Uncollected)

Pensive, he can distil a mood, and like Vijay make the commonplace precious.

and we must forget,
the short hide seek we played,
and just know,
this is once again wind flower season,
there'll be bright periwinkles soon all over us again,
or perhaps, if the mud is not just right,
just the parenthesis of us naked, staring stone hard,
at the rain...

("Dash")

C P Surendran shows himself in his poems as a bruised self, torn in love and relationships, but the poetry it brings on is poetry on the edge. A sense of heightened awareness especially in retrospect, marks his poems. Often in Surendran, there is an attempt at self-annihilation, or of past memory, though they rebound.

Home, I tell the man turning away in the mirror.
My captive. Let him go?
Cut my wrist and set off a little sunset.
Let him go.

("Back")

Introduction

Boyhood, a sense of failure in emotional bonding, are strong undercurrents in his poetry. Surendran's acumen to create flash-imagery is noteworthy.

> *And, cruelly, no one remembers the enemy,*
> *Or whose turn it's next; from whose chest*
> *Flesh will fly like sparrows from a nest.*
>
> ("Sparrows")

Or, as in

> *The leaves whispering*
> *A wreath around my head,*
> *And watch time toss torches*
> *Through the trees*
>
> ("Self-Recrimination"- Available Light)

'Reflection" a poem ruminating a Mumbai suburban train journey in which the poet observes a man piercing a child with a pin every time it cries, is perhaps one of Surendran's best poems.

> *On the far sea I saw a ship docked*
> *Between two stars, shedding and loading*
> *Its cargo of fireflies. From darkened homes*
> *I heard babies wailing through the night.*
>
> ("Reflection")

C P Surendran captures for us, the universe we often miss in a blink.

Jeet Thayil is of a different cast altogether. His sagacious poems need to be relished in quiet, sipped over and over, letting the taste and the fragrance run around the tasting tongue.

> *The world is code, smoke signals the*
> *dead have left us to decipher, knowing we cannot.*
> *At nightfall, exhausted by toil, he falls deep into the*
> *dreamless light changes, the dead or dying sea.*
>
> ("Self-Portrait")

Jeet's poems in remembrance of Shakti Bhatt are not just poignant. They are heart rending.

> 47. Hi,
> 48. Shakti, it's New Year's Eve, 2007, 5.49
> 49. p.m. We're in a coffee shop in Manali and I'm
> 50. Looking at the ice
> 51. On the Himalayas and writing this line.
> 52. I have no idea at the time
> 53. But in three months to the day you will die.

("53 Views of Abstraction, 1 Rhyme, 0 Blackbirds")

Language is at the same time both quiet and a riot.

> *To imagine the bed you're in,*
> *the vertiginous smile that will break him,*
> *the man whose roses bleed at your window.*

("Separation's Sonnet")

Jeet's poems can also disturb the psyche, with metaphors dense and gumptious.

> *Round the cape of no hope*
> *We awake, you wife, I husband,*
> *Our ship a room of wet rope.*

("The Wedding Picture")

In many of Jeet's poems, a mystery within the poem is the allure. There is revelation as the mystery clears. Consider the poignantly beautiful lines, maturing in their strange simplicity, in the same poem

> *Bees stop, flowers die,*
> *Grief takes its human shape.*
> *These are the signs we make*
> *To know we are alive.*

("Wedding Picture")

Vijay Nambisan, who made his way into Indian English poetry with aplomb with "Madras Central" that spoke of the suddenness of departures and the sense of one filling others' spaces with one's "unwantedness", is right from the beginning talking of relationships, and bonds that turn bitter, burn the heart and die.

> *My mother would frown,*
> *And shake her head, and laugh*
> *.........*
> *And later, sitting by herself in the dusk,*
> *She would be sad awhile.*
> *For my grandfather was once a poet*
> *And some of the world's weight*
> *Had lain upon his shoulders.*

("Poetic Licence")

Alienation recurs in Vijay Nambisan's poems. Perhaps Vijay echoes Gwendolyn Brooks and her statement 'Me happiest when writing poetry'.

For one imbued with unearthly sensitivity as Vijay's, the futility of the earth's blossoming was something Vijay could not ever come to terms with as he observes in "The Miracle of the Pomegranate"

> *But the tree's grown so tall that half its prizes*
> *Will only come to the wasteful bats and thieving*
> *Squirrels, then be left to lose their colours, rotting,*
> *Laying the secret bare to be sympathized with.*

We find Vijay using his gift of his power of observation, to paint his poems on birds, animals, and nature around him, such that poems such as "Snow," and "Cats have no Language", become photo-poems. Nature and the environment become his study room. There is in him a James Wright quality of whom it has been said that he had a "style of pastoral surrealism, built around strong images and simple spoken rhetoric". Whoever thought that ducks could be the theme for enduring poetry?

> *A duck*
> *Maybe thinks she has reason to hide*
> *What she does with her feet. She must float*
> *For no one must know she can walk on water.*

("Double Bill")

In many ways, just as in the gripping letters of the last days of Keats, Vijay's later poems dwell on the theme of helplessness and hopelessness of life in the face of disease and impending death.

> Hold me tight, I pray
> That I may not be compelled to face the worst
> with worser still. What, will this blood be shed
> From mere longing, saying what cannot be said?

("Integument")

Summing up, why this anthology at all? There has been a long felt need to bring poets from the same soil together, such that an anthology of this kind helps to trace roots of being, and to arrive at the sources and thematic structures that make such creative pursuits possible, linking them in terms of perspectives that would help us focus not only on the unity of thought, writing, and theme, but also would help determine the diverse and independent elements that make for such poetry.

Aimee Nezhukumatathil also gives us the hint for the need for such an anthology, already overdue when she wistfully opines in her remembrance lecture on Meena Alexander worthy of reiteration here.

'...... *Kerala, the emerald green, southernmost coast of Kerala, a place I love so deeply in my veins and lungs but never saw in any poems brought into my classes or any book I could find in our suburban libraries.... You have to understand that I made it through twenty years of schooling and no poet from India was ever brought into my classroom. You have to understand, when I saw her use the word Kerala in a poem (long after I finished grad school) I wept....*'

If the above is the emotion of a major poet in the USA with Kerala blood in her veins, on Kerala, the need to have its poets and poetry together as a meaningful collective encompassing the ambient air, justifies itself.

Indian Poetry in English is entering a phase of world acclaim, and region-wise compilation of poetry anthologies from the rest of India in a like manner is the need of the hour to build a treasure house of consolidation of poetry being presently written. Such mirroring of creative writing allows for wider transparencies and mutually inclusive critical appreciation and attention.

This anthology is a first step in that direction.

Gopikrishnan Kottoor

LIVING POETRY

ENGLISH POETRY FROM KERALA
Seven Contemporary Poets

KAMALA DAS

(1934-2009)

Kamala Das grew up in Punnayurkulam village, Thrissur, in Kerala and lived in Kolkatta and Mumbai. Though largely self- taught, her works have attracted world attention for their literary role in setting free, the woman's bonded sexual psyche. Kamala Das, who later converted to Islam, and preferred to be known as Kamala Suraiyya, is also regarded as a major writer in Malayalam. Her notable awards include the Sahitya Akademi Award and Vayalar Rama Varma Award.

    Her works in English include *Summer in Calcutta*, *The Descendants*, *The Old Playhouse and Other Poems*, *Collected Poems*, *Only the Soul Knows How to Sing* and her autobiography *My Story*. At the time of her passing, she lived in Pune, Maharashtra.

March of the Mercenaries

Love was the only religion
I ever recognized. We
arrived with love-words, it became
even more relevant. I made
our anxieties mine, the rhythm
of your breathing, the frequent ache
of your calloused feet, and then
without unease
your religion too.
But very soon
I discovered that Allah was
not your Master; fearing the wrath
of your commanders you left me,
your march was that of a soldier
who belonged to a regiment
of mercenaries, your courage
that of a robot's remotely controlled.
Where is the paradise
we together dreamt of,
gardens filled with nightingales' song,
angels sliding down the blue skies?
I do not any more hold you
in my arms. An ache lives within,
an ache that does not seem to die…
The crumbling of my world thumps
against my ear, the trees descend,
flowers drop, ripened fruits fall
and the nightingales'
nests fill with eggs.
When an egg breaks
I think of a tomorrow
that ends like
a foetus that dies, open-mouthed.

The Magnolia

Like a magnolia bent with
excessive bloom was my frail form
burdened with desire. But
you humbled with coarse words, made
me feel old and inadequate.
I cannot buy youth at any
pharmacist's. Take yourself away
from the sunny orbit of my life,
impotent male who with a grin
of pride calls himself a sadist.
You have sullied the purity
of my perspective. You have slain
love with knife-thrusts of verbiage.
Have I been perverse till now, drawn
to a small-town symbol of fair
commonness, a Palaeolithic
toy made out of clay? Why did
the cranes, their wings agleam, rise
from the ripened rice fields and fly
to dim my landscape and my sky?
Why did a rain of misery
overflow the horizon's rim?
You could not ejaculate but
I ignored the flaw. You spewed
anger, an orgasm singular
and strange. I owe nothing, I don't
owe anybody a thing but perhaps
I do owe something to poetry.
When I walk the nights away
sleepless with a tread lighter than
a soul's, I break the backs of
roaches, the brittle shells of egos,
but that too is a poet's fate.
Illness and medications sprout
a kind of verse oddly perfect.

One gets only the hell well deserved,
thank God for that. My lover
is a chess piece I must sweep off
the board to bring order where
disorder roams. I shall not have
a heavy hand on my bosom,
a greying head against my knee,
I shall no longer feel thirst or
hunger. I shall swallow gusts of
sweet air and chew down the slats of
yellow, yellow, yellow sunshine...

The Sensuous Woman

The sensuous woman must choose her illness as she
Chooses her clothes to suit her own style, a certain
Delicate condition invisible to the eye
Inspiring awe and tender sympathy
So that she may lie, a martyr's halo
Lighting up her pillowcase, under rugs
Of cashmere or silken quilts, limbs flaccid
As a baby's skin, cool as a rose, and
The visitor tiptoeing in with his
Offerings of flower or fruit must inhale
The sandal in the air, the scent of cotton wicks
Burning themselves out in lamps which her room
Mysteriously seems to hold always,
Although bare of such exotica, and must stoop
To kiss the back of an idle hand, unused
To chores all except that of kindling love.
And, as day and night as one tide after
Another roll away, an ocean's vast
Languor seizes her blood, the fences between
The state of life and death fade, and nailed
To the pleasant cross of Being she straddles
The handless clockface of eternity.

Scalpels

You gave me no wedding ring
or even a promise laced with hope
You held me in your arms
and passed on your cough to me
After half a year has passed
the cough still lingers on:
 Love too endures, I hope…
On the phone at your hospital
your voice, a steely scalpel
probing my innards,
drives me to the farthest
periphery of your world
I shiver like an outcaste
I taste the cold metal of defeat
Perhaps only in my arms
you soften
adopt a human form
At such moments you serve me
ladles of silence
in a leisurely way
the silence of old trees
adorning your family home
which remember you as a child
the silence of birds that roost
invisibly in the trees
the silence of distant hills
in the wake of a storm.

I Dare Not Gaze Again

Don't turn your face
or look at me, dear one
I dare not gaze again
into the depth of sequestered pools

Behind the layers of cold skin
may lurk sleeping suns
that might rise out of the water
like naked leprechauns
to beguile
to please
I dare not play the games
adults seem to play
the game of enticement
the game of laughter
and the final one of abandonment.

The Maples Are Green Still

Perhaps in slumber lies
as yet unemerged
the tarnished copper of their leaves
and my beloved's too
I remember the red hot rages
that awakened
under my gypsy lips.
Was there ever a woman
able with words to describe the
splendours of her
lover's body?
Ya Allah
import for us
for my silent one and me
from the heavens above
a language that is versatile
and conveys love's anguish
and the concomitant bliss
with words that resemble the sighs
of moments when we cling
and afterwards uncling
in leisurely detumescence

Ya Allah
I thank you once again
and again and again
For this gift of a man
who is now my sustenance
the draught I thirsted for
and the sole raiment
for my nudity, both my body's
and my soul's.

A Feminist's Lament

An ideal woman, they said, was but
a masochist. Trained from infancy
to wear the flannels of cowardice
next to her skin, trained to lie inert
under a male, committed by vows
to feed her, clothe her and buy for her
the 1000 sq. ft. flat with a loft
for storing the debris of passing years.
I was never that ideal dream. Nor
did he buy the flat for me.
Widowed and diabetic
wrinkling like a bitter gourd
not even death can perfect me now.
What was courage worth
at the very end?
Even Phoolan the dacoit queen
finally threw down her guns
to settle for weekly orgasms.

Larger than Life Was He

The living must ultimately
triumph over the dead
and outlive them in moderate calm,
In twenty weeks
my grief gave way to faint stir-
rings of guilt.
In the gauzy sleep of dawn
I had not lain against him
for fifteen years or more
I had tried as satiated wives did
to wean him off desire
My celibacy flowed like a river in spate
between the twin beds in our room
There are no memories that enthral,
no fond phrase capsuled in thought,
It was never a husband and wife bond.
We were such a mismated pair,
Yet there were advantages, I admit
He was free to exploit and I was free
to be exploited.
We were quits at every game we played
I could have been Sita to his Rama
had I been given half a chance.
I reared three sons,
he was too busy to watch them grow
but he it was who wore the faded face
that they recognised as their father's.
His was the heavy tread
heard on the gravel at dusk
He peered into his office files
till the supper turned cold
and the children got up to sleep
I cannot recollect a film
a play or a concert he took us to
or a joke which together we shared.

He was like a bank locker
steely cold and shut
or a filing cabinet that
only its owner could unlock
Not for a moment did I own him.
Only a few bed-bound chores
executed well, tethered him to me.
Emotion was never a topic
brought up in our home
although for long it remained
as grist for the tales that the night
and I, combined, produced.
Do I miss him?
Of course, I do, for larger than life
was he. I miss that brusque voice
sending out the trays
hugging their manuscripts
meekly as unwed mothers did
their illegitimate offspring
I miss his censoring my daily mail
his screening each phone call
and the insulation of his care.

Too Late for Making up

Father, it's too late for making up with you
The time for debates on honour is over now
You won, didn't you? You left me without goodbye
Or a look that told of your feelings for me.
All I could do was light an oil lamp
And place it beside your head
After they had wrapped you in off-white khaddar
And laid you on our drawing room floor.
Everyone who knew you brought you a wreath
Either of lilies or of rose,
At last to spare your tired legs I cried

Leave them standing against the wall.
You turned cold on the drawing room floor
Colder than your heart ever was, father.
The house was filled with red-eyed people
And someone read the Gita
Some weeping would have looked real nice
It is done in the best of families you know.
All I could do was sprinkle eau de cologne on you
And decorate your chest with flowers,
She is the daughter that went astray
I heard someone whisper
The one who caused him the greatest pain
And look at her now, acting solemn.
Should I have loved you, father
More than I did
That wasn't so easy to do
If I have loved others, father,
I swear I have loved you the most.

The Maggots

At sunset, on the river bank, Krishna
Loved her for the last time and left.
That night in her husband's arms Radha felt
So dead that he asked, what is wrong,
Do you mind my kisses, love? and she said,
No, not at all, but thought, what is
It to the corpse if the maggots nip?

The Anamalai Poems

I

How often have I trod these mountain paths,
The mist, like tattered pennants beckoning
to me; yes, from each city I lived in,
each dusty small town I stole out often
to walk this winding road, laying aside
my poor body that had perhaps no home,
no territory to call its own. Mine
was a somnambulistic tread, so soft
that not even the labourers heard it,
who walked with hooded heads among the trees.
There was none to see me or recognise
but the bird hidden in the silver oaks
a bird that cried out my name, a shrill cry
that pierced the silent sombre fog slowly
ascending the lone Anamudi peak...

II

There were nights when I heard
my own voice call me out
of dreams, gifting such rude
awakenings, and then
expelling me from warm
human love, unaccustomed
fare for one such as I,
a misfit when awake.

III

If I had not learnt to write how would
I have written away my loneliness
or grief? Garnering them within my heart
would have grown heavy as a vault, one that
only death might open, a release then

I would not be able to feel or sense...

IV

Ultimately we come to know
that for us there is only one
claimant whom by mistake we call
death, obsessed as we are by our
physicality, restrained
by the eyes' inadequate power
to perceive beyond the farthest
precincts of truth. If only the
human eye could look beyond the
chilling flesh, the funeral pyre's
rapid repast and then beyond
the mourner's vanquished stance, where would
death be then, that meaningless word
when life is all that there is, that
raging continuity that
often the wise ones recognise as God?

V

At times I feel that I hide behind my dreams
as the mountain does, behind the winter's mist
I cannot look the day in the face as once
I did, with gumption or confront myself and
declare, yes, old girl, I have sure let you down.
They called me a winner, for, with words I did
weave a wondrous raiment fit for Gods and with
nimble footsteps climbed the stairways of my thoughts
finding even the heaven's portals ajar.
My songs echoed in stranger's dreams, in unease
they stirred in their sleep and sighed. Yes, often, poets
gatecrash into the precincts of others' dreams
as Gods and Goddesses do many a time in unsolicited
        magnanimity.

VI

    I have cut myself adrift from those who professed
    to need my love and can now have freedom even
    if it be that insecure one of the boat
    bereft of rowers, oars or sails, yes, only
    the blood's moorings have any relevance but
    they rest in ancient graveyards now turned into
    municipal playgrounds where over layers
    and layers of brittle bones the booted legs
    of adolescents kick a football around
    or, in the southern wing of the ancestral
    estate where the coconut trees have nailed down
    the matriarchs' bosoms with thirsting roots.
    No, not for me the beguiling promise of
    domestic bliss, the goodnight kiss, the weekly
    letter that begins with the word dearest,
    not for me the hollowness of marital
    vows and the loneliness of a double bed
    where someone lies dreaming of another mate
    a woman perhaps lustier than his own.

VII

    If someone would only remove the sun
    from my way I would not have to face
    another sorrowful day but I would
    lie then in kind night's embrace, soothed by its
    blinded compassion while its groping fingers
    would anaesthetise my private terrors…
    If someone would coax the night to linger
    beyond its legitimate phase, I shall
    not wake with tear filled eyes again or look
    down the chasm of another sad day
    to perceive each and every time only
    the debris of the past night's genial dreams.

VIII

> The longest route home is perhaps
> the most tortuous, the inward
> path you take that carries you step
> by weary step beyond the blood's
> illogical arrogance, yes,
> beyond the bone and the marrow
> into that invisible abode of pain,
> yes, that deathless
> creation tethered to your self,
> and constantly struggling to wrest
> itself free, tethered to your soul
> as your shadow is to your form,
> your Siamese twin no surgeon
> can cut away from you. Other
> journeys are all so easy but
> not the inward one, the longest
> route home and the steepest descent...

IX

> Life yields its true meaning only
> in early youth or in weary
> age. The middle is an opaque
> glass pane, muddied by finger-prints.
> In meaninglessness, trapped, I must
> so remain and taste the outer
> rind of human pain and the seeds
> of mirthless laughter.

X

There is a love greater than all you know
that awaits you where the red road finally ends
its patience proverbial; not for it
the random caress or the lust
that ends in languor.
Its embrace is truth and it erases
Even the soul's ancient indentations so that
Some unknown womb shall begin to convulse
To welcome your restructured perfection.

ANNA SUJATHA MATHAI

(1934–

Anna Sujatha Mathai was born Nagpur, Maharastra, but would hop over every two years to her village town of Tiruvalla, Kerala. She studied at universities in Delhi, Edinburgh, Bangalore, and Minnesota. Her poetry collections include *Mother's Veena, Life on my side of the Street,* and *The Attic of Night.* She has been published in the Penguin book of contemporary Women poets edited by Arlene Zide. Her work has appeared, among others, in London Magazine, Poetry Review, UK, and The Illustrated Weekly, India. Her work appears in Post-Independence Poetry by Indians in English edited by Arundhathi Subramaniam. She lives in New Delhi.

Living Poetry

Perfume

One whose sorrows
    had turned into dark mines
    within her, so that she had
    become as rigid as coal.

Once, her being had grazed
    the edge of freedom,
    of a possible love,
    but duty had drawn her back
    to a soulless charade.

Her husband, her sons,
    later, her daughters-in-law,
    felt stifled by her laws and rules.

There was cruel talk
    when the sons sought
    to make their own marriages,

But found themselves
    in warped situations
    with no hope.

The day she died,
    her daughters-in -law
    opened her cupboard and discovered
    a cache of the finest perfumes.

Perfumes that would have
    shed their beneficence
    upon their twisting,
    twisted lives.

They flung open the bottles,
    so carefully saved.
Not a drop of fragrance.
All dry.
If only, like Mary Magdalene,
She had opened the bottles
And spread the perfume all around—
    if only—

Out of Reach

The essence of a perfume
Always evades us.
Surrounded by abundance of life
We find ourselves alone.
Why can't we throw ourselves
Into the dance,
With the dancers?
Why can't we sing
In ecstasy with the singers?
Why does colour surround us
So tantalizingly,
And yet we can't touch it or hold it.
We stay thirsty in
A world full of oceans and rivers.
Are we always to be hungry, thirsty
At this feast of life?
When shall we sit down
At the table of life
And rise with our hearts full?

Anna Sujatha Mathai

Coming Running Jumping

(For Craig Raine, British poet, who told me he had asked a man at Gandhi's burial place, what "He Ram" meant. The man had replied "That guy he done shoot me dead." Raine thought writers here should use more of the language spoken by people around them.)

The day I came home, in the afternoon,
small son in tow—we'd just had lunch,
fried fish and rice, sitting in the school garden—
we were met by old Angela at the door.
Black and wrinkled, the fake diamond
nose-ring and ear-rings glittering
wickedly—she'd got them from the pawn shop—
her nephew had his eyes on them, she said.
"Where's master?" I asked. She smiled—
that coy little-girl smile. Her blouse,
full of safety pins and faded mangal sutras,
jiggled in indignation. "Madam", she replied,
"What I do? You no come.
Master coming early from the hospital,
He taking big bag full of bumps—
(My Italian bag, I thought. He always claimed
it brought him luck.)—and taking
so much money" (she held her arms apart,
a little girl clutching
a large bag of sweets)—
"he put it in the bag. He coming,
running jumping down the stairs.
He closing garage door and putting suitcase in the car.
He no say goodbye.
Master very naughty man."
Angela, being deaf, didn't hear my gasp.
He'd left only his torn sandals behind.
Not a note, or a message for the child.
Angela knows about long silences and loneliness—
she has only that nephew,
who covets her nose-ring.

"Who care for me when I be old?
Who bury me when I die?"

My Lost Language

I search for my lost syllables
In the green grass of the paddy fields.
My lost language, Malayalam,
Has dropped like a gold wedding band,
Which slipped off the finger
Into the stream below,
A lost bond lying
In the flowing water,
Amid the pebbles deep in the water.
As I search, I hear my grandmother's voice
Speak from the bed under the attic stairs.
How many nights I lay with her
Sharing the pain and the sorrows of her life.
The smell of whole mangoes pickled in brine
Emanates from the earthen *bharanis* lining the wall,
Vying with the smell of jasmine
Coming in through the open window.
Grandmother smells of aromatic oils
Meant to ease her pains.
In the dark night outside, snakes shed their skin.
I hug her tight as she tells me
In the music of that lost language
About her sad childhood,
The cruel stepmother, the hunger, the humiliation,
The struggle to learn a little English,
All in Malayalam, which opens windows.
On the day of her death she appears to me in a dream.
Clear bells ring, piercing my consciousness.
Molle, you know I lived a sad life,
But can you feel it now, the joy?
She holds out the lost band to me—
English and Malayalam bound together in gold.

My lost language shines in the palm of my hand,
Forming intimate syllables.
Rediscovering lost memories,
A language that trembles in my deepest sleep.

Ishvari's Voice

Ishvari used to lie down
on a mat in my room at night.
Unbinding her long hair,
Loosening the folds of her *mundu*,
Shaking out the grass mat,
And sighing, after the long day,
She'd speak to me
Or perhaps to anyone out there in the night.

She spoke of her lovers,
Of the one who had killed himself,
his beautiful body with the lights of his male desire
Put out for ever.
Of the babies who lay dead—
'Lovely fair babies, Ama,
boys left to die by the hospital gates.'
Unwanted babies, illicit desires.
Is desire ever illicit? Are babies ever illegitimate?
Those lovely 'boy babies', some girls too
Why did they die?
If you touch the raw edge of life's jagged surfaces
You get wounded.
Out there it's dark.
The cobra lays eggs
Which ensure another generation.

The retina of night is unflickering
Ishvari, domestic servant, has known it all.
Abandonment. To be abandoned.

Her eyes—cold and indifferent in the daytime
Become phosphorescent at night
      —like a cat's.

Stones

Stones lay upon her eyes
and each day tears fell
upon her face, a river bed
with fine lines carved by misery.
The river's direction was lost.
Once it had moved to the open sea;
now it was a stagnant pool
with no horizon.

She remembered lost youth, lost chances—
and fretted in her prison,
bearing the life sentence to hard labour.
The children were leaving her—
gay and careless as autumn leaves
that fall from the trees.
How could they know the tree's pain?

Her husband stood apart, and their hands
could not touch, could not comfort,
Night had come, and her eyes
had turned to stone.

Life is a kind doctor who gives us death
in small daily doses
so that when at last, we drink
death's dark wine,
we have already tasted its bitterness.

On the Beach at Baga

The fishermen cast their nets
        into the living sea,
        and churn out death.
No death is painless
        or without blood,
for the white fish are
        bleeding out their lives
        on the white sands,
haemorrhaging soundlessly
        as their guts rip
and they gasp their last
        breath of sea's foam.

On the sands of Baga
        where the bay converges
        with the red ore hills,
the sun dips with violence
        every evening.
But it is not the sun,
        not the sun,
but the world that is wheeling,
quite indifferent to the fish,
        the people, the living things,
that are caught in its crevices
        and fissures.

No, it is not the sun that is
        bound upon night and day
        and ceaseless alternation.
The sun has only the memory of flame
        and for centuries has watched
        the earth dance like a clown
        upon one foot,
someday it will drop and die,
        laughing, laughing madly.

On the beach of Baga
      a hippie woman reels
holding a small golden baby,
dropping him, and gazing out
      upon the sea,
remembering lovers that have left,
leaving her only with
      the cry of a child.
Lonely eyes, wild and dazed,
      watch the sun set
and the baby knows again
      its mother's alternating moods
      of warmth and cold rejection.

Oh the fish are dying
      on the beach at Baga,
the sting-ray sleeps with
      the small gentle fish
and all things are equal in death.
But the fishermen have
      warm eyes and full stomachs.
They have salted the fish
      and are ready for the night voyage.
Small boats on the enormous sea,
with some luck they will see
      the daylight creep in.

Song of the Fall

Leaves fall from the trees
Stunning me with their brilliance.
I run to the window,
      leaning out
Rapturous at that beauteous fall.
Freedom is leaves falling, I cry,

Yellow and red and amber
And tender green.
Freedom is a road flashing
      before me,
A road of mystery.
I say goodbye to mother
I'm a big girl now.
But the falling leaves
      strike me with terror—
This is not beauty, but bareness.
I run from the window,
Fearfully crying—
'Leaves. Return to your trees.
How lovely you were when
      You stood there quiet,
Ordinary tree, with ordinary leaves'
Father said, 'You're an ordinary flower,
You must fit in'.
I've been such a misfit,
Ordinary beauty escaped me.
Tree of extraordinary beauty,
Road of the miraculous turn,
Freedom the vanishing leaf,
Bright image within me,
Falling earth upon me
Help me to bear the fall.

In Tiruvella

My grandmother's grave has no flowers upon it.
They have built a railway line close by.
The trains rush past in the fields
Where we walked as children.
Even death has not parted my grandparents
Though life did,
and their graves touch

though they never were close in life.
In the house where they lived
the jackfruit and the temple flowers have withered,
the coconut trees yield less fruit.

Often my sister and I would sit
On the black marble parapet
Of the verandah in that house,
And suddenly notice grandmother's violent signals to
      us
    from behind the door.
She never thought it seemly
    that we young girls
Should sit and argue with grandfather
In the presence of other men.
We were growing up now, she reminded us,
And would soon be married, if we were lucky.
I asked my grandfather why girls can't do anything.
My wonderful, kind grandfather comforted me, and
    said
Men would adore me when I grew up.
Grandmama said: Get her married
before the light goes out of her face.
What was it, this light, in my young face
And what put it out?
'Grandpapa knows nothing of life,'
My grandmother often insisted,
'If it weren't for me he would be completely cheated.'
When we came from the city she insisted we were filthy
Because we never had oil baths, and scrubbed us with
    inja.
We loved to help her draw water from the old well,
And hang dangerously over the edge
Watching our own reflections.
Grandfather lived in his study,
piled high with wonderful-smelling old books,
She in the kitchen, cooking and scrubbing.

Once I wanted to get her a gold-bordered *kashava*
      *kauni**
But she said she was too old for such frivolities.
She had been beautiful once,
but had been married at eleven,
to a man whom she did not find handsome.
She never loved his face as we did, dear kind
      old grandfather.
Yet it was he who helped her learn enough English
to wade through the works of Dickens and Thackeray.
At night, the still musky nights,
When the snakes shed their skins upon the red earth
      outside,
Grandmother would ask toothless Kurumba Chovathi,
Her companion since they were seven,
To massage her aching legs.
She would say 'Kurumbe, tell the child
of the solid gold chain I wore on my hip'
But her cruel step-mother had removed it
When she got married.
Once my grandmother said to me
Don't tell anyone, but
I don't think there is any God.

After I got married I never saw my grandfather.
Blind by now, he still wrote loving letters,
Full of his yearning to see us.
After six years abroad I got a telegram,
And we travelled to Tiruvella.
A snake crossed our path
      just as we were approaching the old house.
He had died an hour before we arrived,
and his forehead was cold when I touched it.
That morning he had said,
'Give me my glasses. The
      children are coming.'
I think the wind in the casuarina trees wept.

Grandmother in her despair could only say,
'Grandpapa always knew where the stamps were kept.'
A year later, my grandmother came to me in a dream,
And held me in a tight embrace.
I could hear pure, clear bells ringing,
and was filled with a great ecstasy.
She said You know I was never happy.
But now I know this great joy. Can you feel it?
And I could. I was filled with peace.
When I heard she had died that evening
I was serene.

So the generations pass.
And the old house in Tiruvella
     is faded now.
We too will fade and die, and our lives
     remain a mystery.
Shall we, in death, lie close
To those our hearts have loved?

*Kashava Kauni—gold-bordered half sari worn over the white lungi and blouse of the Syrian Christian women of Kerala.

Light

When I was seventeen
And dreaming of distant lands
And faraway loves,
My grandmother said
'Get her married
   before the light
      goes out of her face.'
The light in a woman's face
Should not be so brief.
It's meant to last a long time,
Nourished by the soul.

Well, they got me married,
and put out that light,
But I learnt to live in candle-light
When the other lights went out.
One learns by subtle contact to reach
Electricity at most mysterious levels.
Light goes from the face, but
Survival lends one light
    that shines most brightly.
She who seeks light,
Must learnt to walk in the darkness,
On her own road.

Frozen

Love is a small space in the sun
In freezing weather,
And to be pushed out of that small,
    saving space
Is the beginning of the death count…
Being frozen to death.

Only the smile on the face
Of the frozen person
Will tell those who care to look,
About the hopes of spring,
How bright they were.

Goddess Without Arms

My poetry didn't come
    full-blown,
a perfect flower,
every petal proudly placed.

It was never a goddess
      rising from the waters
seated serenely on a shell,
or emerging from a lotus
      all her arms gracefully extended,
a Canova Venus or a Saraswati,
resplendent in her plenitude,
      certain of her sovereignty.
No. It grew painfully,
      armless,
      limbless,
      somewhat blind,
      a few stray petals here and there,
      more like wounds.
But day by day,
      inch-by-inch
it gathered grace,
      arms, limbs, eyes…
wholeness.

Mother's Stories

A high-transmitter wire,
humming with stored up
codes, life-capsules from past generations,
Mother is losing her memory,
her memories quick with life,
memories I could dip into,
a granary, a storehouse, rich with stories,
of people and places,
relationships, hates,
loves and jealousies,
pettiness and forgiveness.
Mother's stories are dying—
where will she go with all these stories?
They'll be too heavy for her to carry across—

and where shall I go when they are gone?
Silence and indifference will choke
the richness of that lost community.
Shall I tell you a story?
Do you remember that man, that woman?
Do you know what she said?
Now there'll be blankness—
I'll grope for stories all alone.
Or perhaps some of them will wake up
and talk to me
in the silence of the night
or in the middle of the busy day.

They'll say,
give us some space,
some light,
hang us out to dry,
and see how life will glimmer through
our worn and threadbare fibres.
She's gone now.
Only the hum of the wires
breaks that
silence...

Time and the Woman

A child, she held a perfect flower
in her grasp,
Searching among rocks, she found jewels.—
Some became dreams, some thorns.
But the dream turned to nightmare,
and every day jewels fell
from her helpless hands.
From the ill-set ring, the perfect diamond of language.
Even her name, carved on rocks,
now submerged in the sea.

All day, angels have been
whispering in her ears.
She, a falling leaf, trembling, vulnerable,
clutches at shining motes of dust,
breaking her giddy fall.
She races with Time, her unfailing companion
in that irrevocable flight
from that continual fall.
Time drops like the moon
on a still night
beneath an endless sea.
Her days have become needles stuck in grooves.
The whispering angels cannot alter
that grating sound.
They can only bend the stalks of corn
which part, as she races
towards her dreams,
recognizing them faintly,
races towards them
as they recede.
Time drops grey into her hair
like quiet fall of snow at night.
She stands upon the
threshold of vast steppes
or like one about to be flung
from a mountain-top.
Poised for the last leap,
she becomes an arrow
aimed at the sun.

The Woman Before

As there are those who fill in
the face of a criminal
they've never seen, just by linking
disparate descriptions.

So I fill in her face from the hints
dropped by you and others,
of the woman you loved so long,
the woman you loved before me.
Is she me? Or was I her?
Aren't all women one?
In love don't we lose identity?
Or do we stand shining and apart
with a halo round the head,
scarred and marked
by our love, by the love of
a man for us.

You're Mine, Not Death's

Let me alone, Love,
don't torment me.
Let me die a quiet humane death
in the mid-stream of my days.
Why do you call me
now, in the middle
of the night,
Just when I'd put out
the lights?
Call me with insistent voices
and angel choirs
that sing from profane altars,
and wake the body into
terrible longing?
Leave me alone.
Let me go on my way in peace.
In my youth I sought you,
and you were cruel and visited me
only when I was out,
or trapped beneath the staircase.
I lived then only

with imaginary people.
With Cryano, or Dostoevski's Prince,
with Anna Karenina, or Madame Bovary,
the poet Christ with his
lilies of the field,
more beautiful than all the
glory of kings.
And now you ask me to love
ordinary men,
now that I wear the veil
and wait for my visitor, Death.
Just when I locked my room
and said I'll write, I'm a poet—
I accept that I belong
to that doomed tribe
who bear their pain
like jewels emblazoned on their sleeves.
Just then you come, Love,
and my breasts bloom.
You come tearing at my doors
and you leave dirty footsteps
all over my house.
You have no respect for locked doors
and signs that say 'Don't Disturb.'
Discourteous visitor, be gone.
and if you must come
at least be gentler in your approach.
Don't tear at my being
and make me cry till I ache.
Don't force this cruel love upon me...
I never chose you.
You chose me, as I was writing,
waiting for my last lover,
 dressed all in purple,
with my hair swimming around me,
waiting for my last lover, Death.
You came in that solemn moment,

blindfolded me, and said
'I've come for you.
You're mine. Not Death's.'

The Woman in the Falling House

Woman is the pillar, the step, on which
the house is built.
From her womb, the generations emerge, and yet,
the sons of men, not women, walk upon
the earth and possess it.
Tradition is a tight warp
binding the woman's body, the woman's heart.
Not the living tradition, which nourishes,
but rigid, dead tradition,
like the shroud which binds the corpse,
which makes living corpses
of the vital woman-flesh, woman-spirit.
It dies slowly, this tradition,
slowly, so slowly, like the slow seep of blood
from one bleeding to death.
Father-in-law bangs his fist upon the table
'Rebellion? Let it be in other people's houses,
other people's families. Not ours.
You are the pillar, the step, the earth, the grass
on which our house is built, on which we walk.'

She cries, 'If I am a bondswoman,
how will my children be free?'
She looks around, and sees
the titles have cracked—
the walls are breaking up,
the beautiful house is disintegrating
there's blood on the walls, a fearful spirit within,
corpses under the foundation.
They should have checked before they

laid that lovely floor!
She, the rebel, the white dove, the dreamer,
crushed by the stones falling from the house.
White dove of innocence, who yearned to fly,
but lay trapped, wings broken by falling debris,
becomes a great bird of the skies,
chaste and powerful,
as the house falls away from her,
the pillars, the steps, the earth...

Hysteria

Yes, for centuries we've been mute.
Not that we're dumb, or our
tongues had been cut out. Not
quite. We could prattle alright:
about recipes, about dust,
about our neighbour's daughter,
about our clothes, secrets about
how to stay beautiful, how to
stay young. We knew nursery
rhymes which we lisped to our
children, but never the dark
interiors of those stories, those
lay shrouded in sleep like the
Sleeping Beauty. Yes, we were
sleeping beauties, baby dolls,
we slept while our children
were branded with seals of ownership,
our names taken from us, we smiled
while others filled in forms for us,
others made laws which ruled our lives.
Yes, we were dumb.
except when we cried, which
was often; when we were ravished
as young girls, by strange, brutal men,

when we bore children, and delivered them
in the agony of childbirth. When our husbands
and our fathers, our brothers and our sons,
and even our lovers, if we dared have them,
struck us and betrayed us,
and sold us and wounded us.
We dreamed of gentle hands and loving words,
for were we not the soil filled with the ache
of longing for the seed, but instead we were
coarsely used, our bodies brutalised, our souls numbed.
And even our mothers denied us.
In the hour of darkness, they
cut off our hair, shaved our heads,
burnt us on the funeral pyre,
burnt us in our homes,
our brothers inherited the earth.
We were disinherited of even our smallest
shreds of humanity, the day we were born.
Our parents cursed us. They educated
our brothers, gave them the land
and the houses, and the future,
and the power and the glory.
We were married off, we were mere
pieces of property, passes from one family
to another, to work and to bear children,
or, if we didn't bear children,
to be cursed for our barrenness.
No one looked into our eyes with love.
If they had, they'd have heard our souls talk.
Instead, all they said was
She's hysterical. Women are like that,
especially when they menstruate, especially
when they stop menstruating,
especially as they approach death.

At Least Songs

'Will I leave only this: Like the flowers that wither? Will nothing last in my name—nothing of my fame here on earth? At least flowers! At least songs!'
Aztec Indian Poem

History is always written by the victor.
The myths, the legends,
belong to the survivor
and the ruined city
must bow to him.
The memories of the weak are obliterated.
Where are the dreams of slaves?
Except when they can translate
their dream of freedom
into revolution.
For to all things there is a season—
and even stones tell stories
sing sad and powerful songs.
Revolutions spring from
silent, secret seed.
No oppressor can for ever
hold back the flood.
Even the gentlest voices are clearly heard
on a day when the wind is quiet
and Time stops to meditate.
'Not even songs, not even flowers?' you ask.
Yes, surely. Those sleep in the
wind's hiding places,
and will seize the unexpected moment
with their fragrance,
their still living, poignant voices, -
A massive choir singing forgotten tunes.

Death and the Poet

From his nostrils
The stench of death—
Helpless, as crocuses
Thrusting outwards in Spring.
So, his blood upon the grass,
Like Spring flowers—
Speak of a beauty
That might have been
And perhaps yet will be.
Blood on the snow,
His beauty ebbing
Like a gradual tide
That hints of grandeur
Further out at sea,
Beyond our sight.
His death a cruel mystery,
A ship shattered at sea,
All traces lost.
He shares our common destiny of death.
His life is fragile seed
That seeks root.
A fire burns in his head
A fierce light shines
From his window.
We are all called to the same Festival,
And are but fragments
Falling, bright sparks from a careless hand—
Children, for a brief day in the sunlight
Before the dark waters embrace us.

Living Poetry

MEENA ALEXANDER

(1951–2018)

Meena Alexander was born in Allahabad, India, and raised in Kerala and Sudan. Her collections of poetry, include *Atmospheric Embroidery, Birthplace with Buried Stones,* and *Quickly Changing River.* She won the PEN Open Book Award for Illiterate Heart. She has been Guggenheim Fellow in poetry. She edited *Indian Love Poems.* Alexander's prose includes the memoir *Fault Lines,* the novels *Manhattan Music* and *Nampally Road,* the essay collections *Poetics of Dislocation* and *The Shock of Arrival: Reflections on Postcolonial Experience,* as well as the critical studies *Women in Romanticism: Mary Wollstonecraft, Dorothy Wordsworth and Mary Shelley,* and *The Poetic Self: Towards a Phenomenology of Romanticism.* She was Distinguished Professor of English at the Graduate Center/Hunter College, CUNY until her passing away in 2018.

Living Poetry

Muse

I was young when you came to me.
Each thing rings its turn,
you sang in my ear, a slip of a thing
dressed like a convent girl—
white socks, shoes,
dark blue pinafore, white blouse.

A pencil box in hand: girl, book, tree—
those were the words you gave me.
Girl was *penne*, hair drawn back,
gleaming on the scalp,
the self in a mirror in a rosewood room
the sky at monsoon time, pearl slits

In cloud cover, a jagged music pours:
gash of sense, raw covenant
clasped still in a gold bound book,
pusthakam pages parted,
ink rubbed with mist,
a bird might have dreamt its shadow there

spreading fire in a tree *maram*.
You murmured the word, sliding it on your tongue,
trying to get how a girl could turn
into a molten thing and not burn.
Centuries later worn out from travel
I rest under a tree.

You come to me
a bird shedding gold feathers,
each one a quill scraping my tympanum.
You set a book to my ribs.
Night after night I unclasp it

at the mirror's edge

alphabets flicker and soar.
Write in the light
of all the languages
you know the earth contains,
you murmur in my ear.
This is pure transport.

She Speaks: A School Teacher from South India

(Raw Meditations on Money)

Portions of a mango tree the storm cut down,
a green blaze bent into mud
and they come to me, at dawn

three girls from Kanpur, far to the north admittedly
(we know this from national geography class,
the borders of states, the major cities).

They hung themselves from fans.
In the hot air they hung themselves
so that their father would not be forced to tender gold

he did not have, would not be forced
to work his fists to bone.
So that is how a portion of the story goes.

Slowly in the hot air they swung, three girls.
How old were they?
Of marriageable age certainly.

Sixteen, seventeen, and eighteen, something of that
 sort.
How do I feel about it?

What a question! I am one of three sisters,

most certainly I do not want father to proffer money
he does not have for my marriage.
Get a scooter, a refrigerator, a horde of utensils,

silks, and tiny glittering bits of gold
to hang about my ears and throat.
Gold is labor time accumulated... labor time defined.

Who said that? Yes, I am a schoolteacher, fifth standard
trained in Indian history and geography,
Kerala University, first class first.

The storm tree puts out its limbs and
I see three girls swinging. One of them is me.
Step back I tell myself.

Saumiya, step back. The whole history
of womankind is compacted here.
Open your umbrella, tuck your sari tight,

breathe into the strokes of catastrophe,
and let the school bus wait.
You will get to it soon enough and the small, hot faces.

See how the monsoon winds soar and shunt
tropic air into a house of souls,
a doorway stopped by clouds.

Set your feet into broken stones
and this red earth and pouring rain.
For us there is no exile.

Dog Days of Summer

In the dog days of summer as muslin curls on its own
        heat
And crickets cry in the black walnut tree

The wind lifts up my life
And sets it some distance from where it was.

Still Marco Polo Airport wore me out,
I slept in a plastic chair, took the water taxi.

Early, too early the voices of children
Mimicking the clatter in the Internet café

In Campo Santo Stefano in a place of black coffee
Bordellos of verse, bony accolades of joy,

Saint Stephen stooped over a cross,
A dog licking his heel, blood drops from a sign

By the church wall—Anarchia è ordine—
The refugee from Istria gathers up nails.

She will cobble together a gondola with bits of
        driftwood
Cast off the shores of the hunger-bitten Adriatic.

In wind off the lagoon,
A child hops in numbered squares, back and forth, back
        and forth,

Cap on his head, rhymes cool as bone in his mouth.
Whose child is he?

No one will answer me.
Voices from the music academy pour into sunlight

That strikes the malarial wealth of empire,
Dreams of an old man in terrible heat,

Hands bound with coarse cloth, tethered to a scaffold,
Still painting waves on the walls of the Palazzo Ducale.

Cadenza

I watch your hands at the keyboard
Making music, one hand with a tiny jot,
A birthmark I think where finger bone
Joins palm, mark of the fish,
Living thing in search of a watering
Hole set in a walled garden,
Or in a field with all the fences torn:
Where I hear your father cry into the wind
That beats against stones in a small town
Where you were born; its cornfields
Skyward pointing, never sown, never
To be reaped, flagrant, immortal.

Lychees

Terrace deep as the sky.
Stone bench where I sit and read,

I wandered by myself
Into the heart of the mountains of Yoshino.

In one hand a book, in the other, a bag made of
        newsprint—
No weather-beaten bones here

Just lychees bought in the market,
Thirty rupees per kilogram.

Stalks mottled red tied up with string,
Flesh the color of pigeon wings—

Sweet simmering.
Sunlight bruises air

Pine trees blacken.
Where shall I go?

The Dhauladhar peaks
Are covered in snow.

For My Father, Karachi 1947

Mid-May, centipedes looped over netting at the well's mouth.
Girls grew frisky in summer frocks, lilies spotted with blood.

You were bound to meteorology,
Science of fickle clouds, ferocious winds.

The day you turned twenty-six fighter planes cut a storm,
Fissured air baring the heart's intricate meshwork

Of want and need—
Springs of cirrus out of which sap and shoot you raised me.

Crossing Chand Bibi Road,
Named after the princess who rode with hawks,

Slept with a gold sword under her pillow,
Raced on polo fields,

You saw a man lift a child, her chest burnt with oil,
Her small thighs bruised.

He bore her through latticed hallways
Into Lady Dufferin's hospital.

How could you pierce the acumen of empire,
Mesh of deception through which soldiers crawled,

Trees slashed with petrol,
Grille work of light in a partitioned land?

When you turned away,
Your blue black hair was crowned with smoke—

You knelt on a stone. On your bent head
The monsoons poured.

Hyderabad Notebook

I.

I used to sit in the New Mysore Café, at a cracked
      marble table top
A cup of foaming coffee in front of me,

Notebook open to catch a fruit fly on a smear of honey.
The café is gone, in its place is a Reebok store,

Another shop has plastic dolls with glued on hair
SIM cards, dark glasses, cell phones in tints of the
      rainbow.

In a high room across the road above carts with chaat
        and spiced tea,
Someone sitting in a chair feels he is slowly going
        blind.

Over and over he runs his fingers over a page
Spelling out the names of God

In exquisite script read right to left and back again
As befits divinity.

He edges to the window, trying to peer out
At the gates of the Golden Threshold.

The Nightingale of India grown heavy in her years,
        lived there;
The place became a hospital, then a university

Stacked with students in stained jeans and kurtas,
A man who sold beedis jostling in pale pink packets,

Another who boiled tea in a tin can
With increments of sugar—

The bitterness of black leaves a mess of tannin
Predicting nothing.

II.

Once loitering, notebook in hand,
I saw a girl with a gash on her wrist, skirt wrapped
        tight about her.

She was kneeling at the gates.
Using a twig she drew in the dirt

What seemed to be a round rock with a cleft in it—

Etching it deep, deeper, till the stick snapped

Using the broken bit she made a tree,
Or was it a railway track, a spitting fire, a fountain.

Where she knelt, crushed stones
Endure planetary forms

The Milky Way flattened out, Pluto in darkness.
Fragments of time clung together

The privilege of self-consciousness thrust aside,
Letting us glimpse a natural language

Syntax of flesh and stone and root
Anchoring us to ordinary earth.

III.

On Nampally Road where the booksellers used to be
I stand in the rush of traffic

By ox carts crammed with sugarcane, trucks twanging
        horns,
Ambassadors, Mercedes Benzs, Marutis.

I see tiny boys on bicycles
Milk cans hanging from their handle bars.

Tyres scuff the asphalt, cut free and leap,
Come to rest in jagged loops of motion by ledges of
        marble
Cut from the bowels of courtly houses
Drumbeats of amber in a fruit fly's eye.

From fitful calendars,
Pages marked in red ink drop into luminous air

Together with the wings of flying things so quick to
    die.
Epiclesis—the breaking of bread

And the gathering-in again:
The loneliness of paving stones

Returning us to a dream of love,
And what we did not know we were.

Bright Passage

I.

Grandmother's sari, freckles of gold poured into silk,
Koil's cry, scrap of khadi grandfather spun,
I pluck all this from my suitcase—its buckles dented,
    zipper torn.
Also pictures pressed into an album:
Parents by a rosebush,
Ancestors startled in sepia, eyes wide open,
Why have you brought us here?

II.

Mist soars on the river, my door splits free of its
    hinges:
My children's children, and those I will never see—
Generations swarm in me,
Born to this North American soil, dreamers in a new
    world.
I must pass through that rocking doorway,
Figure out words, clean-minted, untranslatable—
Already in the trees finches are warbling, calling my
    name.

Moksha

I

At the tail end of the year
Leaving the dry season behind,

I saw leaves the color of sparrow's wings
Dissolve into the brickwork of a railway station,

A sudden turn of the head and there she stood
On a dusty platform, wool sweater

Smouldering hair, the familiar heaviness of flesh,
Aged a few years, my sister-in-law

After all the winds of the underworld will do that to
          you,
By her side a suitcase

Glistening leather bound by straps
Inside a packet of powdered rice

A morsel of coconut, three red chillis
Fodder for the household gods.

II

Last night in dreams I watched her
In a crush of women severed from their bodies

Drifting as slit silk might
In a slow monsoon wind.

By her, in a kurta knotted at the sleeves
—who knew that spirits could beckon through clothes-
The one they called Nirbhaya—
A young thing raped by six men in a moving bus

(She fought back with fists and teeth)
Near Munirka bus station where I once stood

Twenty-three years old, just her age
Clad in thin cotton shivering in my sandals

III

Now I hear them sing
In delicate recitative

My sister-in-law and Nirbhaya,
That other, less than half her age,

A song as intricate as scrimshaw
In vowels that flowered

Before all our tongues began,
Their voices

The colour of the bruised
Roses of Delhi.

No Rescue (with Toy Cars)

You thought that by crossing all these seas
Writing all these poems something would happen.
But nothing has happened except that you have grown
Older; that's one part of it, the other the gods know
But keep quiet about. They hide the secret
In their clenched fist
Over and over they fold their muslin
Handkerchiefs, the ones used for waving
Goodbyes. No amount of saffron or incense
Will make them change their minds.

Nor does the peddler help, he cries out in a hoarse
Voice, old man with rusty bicycle toy cars tied to the
Handlebars, tiny plastic things in the grey colours
Of the sea gates of your city.

Sarra Copia accused of Heresy in the year 1641

I am caught in a net of lavender
I am drunk on jasmine
I am charred from the throat down.
Swallows flutter
Where my sonnets were burnt.
Stretch marks on the belly of the sky
Why write that.
What about the incorruptible soul?
How can I defend myself?
You ask me about the soul:
She is the scent of wild violets
She is the humming bird caught
In a rainstorm
She is brazen
As light on a beggar's face
She is the bitter crystal
That never shatters
She is light in the womb
She is the pride of angels
She is a moist palm print
She is a fragrant pubic hair
She is a drop of milk
On my right nipple,
She is all, she is none of the above.
She is the star of Abraham
She is Rachel's gold
Ashes of the holy
Take me home.

Univocity

Word over all, beautiful as the sky!
—Walt Whitman

Provincetown by the Sea

As August fades I pedal hard.
At Angel Food I pick up Portuguese fig cake,

Almonds cut and buried in speckled dark,
Pinpricks of sweetness bound in Saran Wrap.

In the High Middle ages
Theologians mused how angels pranced

On the head of a pin,
How the spirit could spin cocoons of flesh,

Whether a body could be in two places at once.
Almost always

I am in two places at once,
Sometimes in three.

Free me weep me Motherwell by the sea,
Night waves succour you.
You knelt on the floor by the canvas, thrust hard:
I made the painted spray

With such physical force
That the strong rag paper split.

Scrim-Scram of Music

How her wrists hurt when she piano played.
He was new in town, the English doctor

In pith helmet and crisp white shirt.
A brand new cure- He pricked her hard.

Drops of gold made her bones boil,
Tongue flower with blisters.

She was dead in a day,
One month short of fifty.

Moonlight, darkening storm.
Dove sta memoria

I never knew my mother's mother.
In her diaries the recipe for mutton curry

Five cloves of garlic, a fistful of green chillis
Sits athwart Gandhi's injunction to spin-

I have laid out my khadi, washed and ironed it.
Tomorrow when I wear it, the sky will be blue.

Nothing known-
The curse and the blessing

Torn rag I pack around the wound,
Curbing the flow that could kill.

Torn Branches

Grandfather lies in wait for me.
I cannot flee.

My voice is young and burnt
My voice is a brambleberry squashed on stone.

All afternoon I lay curled in a hole
In the bamboo grove where cobras rove.

No one knew.
Rove—How did I learn that verb?

From my Scottish tutor-
She rapped my knuckles hard.

A swan in a bag, worth two in the lake.
A stitch in time saves nine.

She taught me some such things
Who will bring me sweetmeats,

Swirl henna on my palms?
Who strokes sugarcane with kerosene

Binds cords of broken rope?
Dark sisters in the sky, their wings are torn.

They have stumps for wrists.
They sing Hosannas to our Lord.

Ars Poetica

By the crook of my knees
I hang in a mango tree.

The leaves are very green.
I slip a finger under my skirt,

I touch the bark of the tree with wetness.
I write on knobbly bark.

A red ant crawls on my skin.
I turn my face to the sky.

The blue is splattered with white.
I write the sky.

The blue is cut with reddish flecks.
From a great distance, they are calling me.

I am in the green tree
They keep calling my name.

When I hear their voices
My finger threatens to catch fire.

Lines with Red Ants

Somethings have holes in them
Leaves on the mango tree

When sparks fly through
I have a hole in between my legs

I pick red ants off the tree,
I let them crawl over me.

Fire blossoms where they bit.
I liked it when the red ants bit.

Bathtub Blues

At the edge of eleven a child
Crouches in a bathtub

Silver scissors in hand,
Skin trembling under metal.

The first materiality is all we have.
Duns Scotus knew this.

The child meets him in the dark,
His loin cloth was made of glass.

She whispers words she learnt by heart.
The mind, the mind has mountains, cliffs of fall.

He forces her to see
Things that beggar speech

(Will strips of chiffon wrap around bone?)
Doctor Subtilis, please save me!

This is not a Dream

Someone stoops at the edge of a pit
The pit is covered with sticks and leaves

In the park the air is heavy
In the park the air is indigo.

Matchstick blue
The scrawl of circling birds.

The snare of love-
Impossible to crawl through.

Black Sand at the Edge of the Sea

Soon I will be given to earth,
Folded in a death squat

Together with pig marrow
Swan's down, thread-leaves sundew,

Pitchblende sucking bones in.
Where is grandfather now?

My friend says think of old Walt
Bent over his dead enemy-

Touching lips to encoffined flesh.
So where do they live

The twin sisters Night and Death?
Will they wash the ground clean?

Debt Ridden

I.

Who are we?

Something was hopping
Up and down in my throat

    O bullfrog

By the stream
Where I was born.

II.

> How did we get here?
> My mother had a pink
> blouse
>
> Over it her sari.
> Something
>
> Was torn.
>
> At first she owed nothing.
>
> Then the sky put paid to us.
>
> The wind altered itself
> And set us all on fire.

Aesthetic knowledge

These are the practices of bodily art—
Burn an almond, collect the soot, mix it with butter.

Enter a cloud
And things are blotted out, ruins restored

So landscape becomes us,
Also an interior space bristling with light.

Have you seen the calendar picture?
Tears from the domes, like droplets of milk,

So memories consume a broken mosque.
We are creatures of this world,

An invisible grammar holds us in place.

When God shows his face

Even mountains start to blaze.
Burnt rock ground very fine

Becomes surma for the eyes, a divine blessing.
For my Dark Night series I used Sumi ink

Culled from the soot of Japanese temples.
For Nur– my Blinding Light series,
Gold leaf pasted on paper,
Utterly fragile.

Udisthanam

Piercings of sense,
Notes lashing time
Ecstatic self hidden
In the ship's hold

"I" legible
Solely in darkness:
Shot flames,
Anchorage of divinity.

On the South Indian coast
In eighth century heat
Tiruvalla copper plate
Marked the morning hour

Before the sea clamored
And the shadow of the body
Lay twelve feet longer
Than Sita herself,

Littoral burning

With sacred fires—passage
To a kingdom beyond
The peepul trees.

Where are those refugees
Amma did not want me to see,
Gunny sacks and torn saris
Stitched together with cord?

Breath of my breath, bone
Of my bone, dark god
Of the Nilgiris,
Who will grant them passage?

GOPIKRISHNAN KOTTOOR

(1956-

Gopikrishnan Kottoor was born in Trivandrum, Kerala. He won the All India Poetry Prize, (Poetry Society, India) and the All India-British Council (Poetry Society, India and the British Council) Special Jury Prize for his poetry. His poem sequence, *Father, Wake us in Passing*, translated into German, and published in Germany won him a Residency in the University of Augsburg, Germany. Gopi Kottoor attended the M.F.A (Poetry) program of Southwest Texas State University, San Marcos, USA in 2000. Gopi Kottoor has published 15 collections of poetry, alongside drama, literary reviews, novels, and translations. His latest poetry collections include *The Painter of Evenings* and *Descent*. He founded the Journal Poetry Chain. He was former General Manager with the Reserve Bank of India.

Living Poetry

Flamingos, Vashi Creek, New Mumbai

As I cross these backwaters
Shelved in clay,
A tranquil suddenness,
Of miles and miles of pink flamingos,
 Stilled into bright bloody lily buds
 Rooted in meditative silence,
As when poetry,
Is still in a poet's heart,
Before the waking bloom,
The sudden flight.

Mother's Sarees

I

Mother's saree box was peacock blue.
She opened it only on special days.
Like, that summer evening when father came home
            early.
She had her bath spread with white jasmine buds he'd
            bought from Nur Jehan Flower Stall
By Old Delhi railway station.
The Regal Cinema near Jama Masjid was playing the
            new black and white talkie
Starring Dev Anand and Suraiya.
Mother liked me to sit by her side, listening to her story
            of each saree
Tucked closely in like an unroused peacock feather.
The jasmine fragrance had already soaked her hair, as
            she laid out the saris one by one
In a semi-circle not unlike a low dipped peacock tail.

Living Poetry

'Which one dear?' she asked me eagerly, 'Which one
 tonight?'
My sleepy eyes dyed down on her Banarasi, Mughal-A-
 Azam Qawwali, Bengal Baluchari,
And Lucknow Chikankari. 'Or, shall it be your father's
 favourite Kashmiri Chinar?'
Sure, each had a story. Each one was a legend.
'This, my son', she whispered 'is the rainbow saree, a
 gift from your father, from Kolkata,
On Durga puja night.... Ah, he has now forgotten. And
 this is the Kancheevaram sari,
Studded with real gold that your father wished me to
 wear on our Kerala honeymoon.
He said I looked like... Shakuntala.... And this is my
 wedding saree.'
Mother kept opening and closing its rummaging silk as
 though helping boneless wings to fly.
I saw her stare hard at the pair of diamonds pinned on
 it,
That had come along with her as dowry.
And I thought I saw tears that she quickly brushed
 aside. We did not choose that.

Mother wore a simple blue that night.
I watched her dress carefully before the long dusty
 bedroom mirror, folding the blue pleats
 peacock crown like, just hovering below her
 navel, as though she remembered the peacock
 dance.
I heard him call her from down below. He had already
 started the car engine.

II

When they came up the stairs to the stairs to the terrace
The moonlight lay already unsheathed.
Mother made sure I was asleep, (or so she thought),

As father's hand slipped over her peacock pleats,
    drawing her close,
Sinking the fangs of the celluloid's black and white
    romance into her flesh
With his lips whorled upon her peacock crown.
Her eyes closed. She lay awake, looking through his
    kisses
At the full moon, thinking perhaps, of King Dushyanta,
    and his fish gobbled ring.

III

Next morning, father took with him in his office jeep,
Mother's tousled saree to Maharani Dry Cleaner's close
    to Nur Jehan Flower Stall.
The blue sari would get back into the blue box in the
    evening,
Among the others awaiting their late night show,
When white jasmine buds would once again spread the
    bath floor.

Vagator Beach, Goa

There's a crucifix
Near the seashore,
Of a boy who drowned,
And I hug it.
Christ never felt so close, so human,
So warm.
I think of him drowning,
His body washed ashore
For a sea side burial.
Late that night I see the last man in the bar
Dwelling in fish
Shrunken omelette, and rain.
There's music,

I'm drowned in already,
That song.
It must be the Pussy Cats.
My friend tells me
Let's get back to Yellow House.
One more drink,
And
My boy, my little boy swallowing the Goan sea,
The whole of it
As
I start the scooter
Hugging
His crucifix.

Mumbai Blasts

I'll not write about the Mumbai blasts.
I'll only write about the 50 pigeons that died
because the fakir who used to feed them grain by the
       Taj Mahal Hotel
was blasted away, and they all died of hunger and
       sorrow.
I'll only make a passing reference to the paupers, the
       begging children,
the hawkers, the sex workers out on an afternoon stroll
and of Boxer, the handsome stray dog that used to come
       for his snooze
at about 1.00 p.m. daily,
his head stoned upon the lap of Gateway of India
and who now, has vanished without a trace.
Thank you, godmen, for your afternoon shower,
and for the embryo still bleeding in its small pool of
       blood,
up the hundred stone steps,
at the lit feet of Mumbai Devi.

From 'Father, Wake us in Passing'

i. America

Did you say
I would come to your arms in December?
And on the phone you asked me,
"Son, what is there in America?"
Father, in America,
The Fall is now breathless beauty.
Tall cypresses draw crimson upon their leaves,
The boughs bend low
Looking for the beauty of blood
In their own reflection
By the water's edge.
Maple leaves fall
With a redness of cheeks around the blaze of strange
        funerals
Holding mist with a wetness of tears.
And this Fall, in America,
I hear the bat wings of your voice on the wires
Shredding to pieces,
Dripping every ray
Of the topaz shedding sun.

ii. Telephone Call

There is a telephone call.
It comes from across the Atlantic Ocean.
You talked then, oh, you tried,
Your voice slurr'd
Dropping to a side.
It wasn't a bit like you. But you said, son,
I must sleep now.
Then you turned over
Late that night, dipping your head onto a pillow of
        stars,

Your brain entangling the milk way,
While I walked out into a misted Fall morning
On the other side of the earth,
The rain pouring entirely
Out of my empty hands.

iii.   Prison House

This is the kindest prison house we have.
Satin white beds.
There, on that one, at the far end,
One sleeps like a log,
With tubes pushed in through the holes in the face.
There again, one pulls at the drip tubes
With a memory of guitar strings.
That's where pain penetrates
Like Sappho said
'Drop by drop'.
Strapped and tied to our walls of pain
Is a sleeping child.
In this kind prison house
Flesh makes no sense. And here is father.
Love laid naked
Upon tips of weathering bone,
A darkness.
Of abandoned light.

iv.   Nectar of the Gods

The nurse hands me a sealed bottle.
'We need a spinal fluid examination on your father'.
I keep the small bottle
In my right pocket.
In the lab they check for final payment,
And I unwrap the cover
On instructions.
For the first time I see your cerebro-spinal fluid, father.

Clearer than tears,
Pure as deep mineral springs,
I hold in my hand,
Stare, at the secret nectar of the gods.

    v.   **Lone Ranger**

The television goes on and on.
The Sunday newspaper with your favourite Jiggs and
    Maggie
Comic strip lies in a corner.
On the teapoy, your spectacles lie open
Like far away twin stations
Awaiting the slow train of your blank eyes.
Remember, you once said,
You would never need such things?
That was before
Words began to fade in your eyes.
The pills that you kept rolling in your hands
Just as your meninges rose inflamed,
The phenobarbitone tablets you thought
You had popped into your mouth,
They still lie under your bed.
The stills of our smiling gods are everywhere on the
    walls
Your bedpan is a white dove of peace,
As you dip alone
Into late streams of silence
Riding far into the sunless hills,
Lone Ranger.

    vi.   **Gift**

I have now set out to do the things
You loved most about me.
About a gift called poetry.
Never wrote like this before,

Perhaps, never again must.
Writing about pain,
Is cruel.
I have set about writing,
What you perhaps would most love me to do–
Write about you.
I am doing that, father.
But it is a kind of way neither of us
Dreamt we would ever do;
For you hold my hand
And I write on.
Though you cannot now lift your little finger,
Through me,
You flow.

vii.   ICU

If I must see you, father, again,
I must peep in through the glass hole of the ICU.
Our second home.
How many such homes do we have to cross?
I go back to your room.
Sit by your empty bed,
Where your dog sleeps by your mattress
Wondering where you have gone.
I must go to mother
To pasteurize her tears.
Read together 'The Buddha and The Mustard Seed'.
I must open the Bible
Heavy with hammerings,
Driving iron nails
Upon Golgotha
Past midnight.

viii. The Colours of Pain

The way your flesh is now pinned down.
The have cut through your spine,
Aspirated your bone marrow,
Sucked your leftover blood
Like benign bats, looking for this and that.
They now say you are worrying them too much.
Take for example, the atrophy in your brain.
Your sensorium –
That shows no sign of return.
Your body, the reminder
Of an Auschwitz clip,
Your flesh that covered me once
In fine cool flannel
Your mouth that called me son
Now sealed off and banded to make room
For the ventilator.
The nurse stacks your blood specimens
By the window,
One upon the other,
As the morning sun warms tenderly
The distant colours of your pain.

ix. Angels on the Moon

Father, you belonged to the black and white era.
You roared with a drone of a world war 2 plane
Over our childhood sky,
And shone like our brightly laced Murphy radio.
Now you have turned into a dark catamaran
drifting alone across the tsunami
Of our star-crossed waiting.
Remember once,
When the two of us went out together
In the cold night rain?
You lit your Players

Sending tiny curls of smoke
Whiter than the small white roses
In our night garden,
Their petals shining like shed wings
Of crying angels on the moon.

    x.   **Sea Crabs**

The night the two of us
Walked the late beach sands.
Dark waves hit the inland rocks
That withstood the water-slaughter
With an inner calm.
The moon was polaroid, giving us instant memories.
Tiny bubbles played flying saucers
Landing on alien planets
Before drifting back to sea.
Deep into the water holes on the ancient sands,
Dark crabs that the sea cast away went scampering to
        hide
Like running griefs of night.
Tonight after all these years,
Those crabs we then chased together
Have come out of their holes, father,
And are running wild,
Wild, wild, all over the lone night beach,
The moonlight hung dead upon their blind eyes.

    xi.   **Wedding Night**

Tonight is your wedding night.
Mother is trembling to fire.
Ashes blow down my face
With the speed of birds
Flying past church bells
Fearing a funeral storm.
Ancient crosses uproot

Spilling over to bleed,
Past this simple tryst you made
Downhill,
Where I fall down to rest,
Beside your crystal salts that press
Hung in great white palls of yesterday and tomorrow
In silent flow, past the half-awake sleeping hamlet of
        your face.

Visiting the Institute of English, 40 Years Later.

Nothing much has changed.
The walls, the old walls, they still hold
The dust of our gone voices,
In memory flakes, we will secretly own,
But will publicly disown.
I go out and photograph the red date palm seeds. I
        remember them,
In my dreams they came back
As her red ear studs.
The same wooden steps, that at times,
Seemed worthy to be made noise of,
But mostly were tip toed by.
There, upon one of them,
Where I intersected her
And gave her my first love letter.
Nights and nights of mountain heaps of her,
In that closed envelope, that she took,
Saying she would not read it,
And would tear it.
But she held it as she ran down the wooden steps,
        making noise,
She held it like she never held me
In her mulberry hand. The same steps,
That she climbed daily,
In and out of my life.

And that hall. Where Dr. Paniker,
 Read out to us, from Dickinson,
And Robert Frost, Because I could not stop for death,
Or, Of mending walls. How he went away,
His lungs choking him in,
Oxygen, oxygen, all around,
But not a whiff to breathe,
Cruel, like a tender poem,
The clasps, and never leaves.
That bright lad, Gopal, with the pig tailed girl
Following him, who topped the Civils,
Was our secret hero,
And who died of kidney failure.
The calm professor Valentine.
That handsome Mohammed
Who thought all the girls where after him
As he lectured to us on Tristam Shandy.
Well. The same trees. The mangoes
Turning ripe in another spring.
The young girls, the new boys,
Playing truant with time and goodbye
Secret love letters wet
In their brightening eyes,
Time that never stops playing,
A dying Keats and his Fanny Brawne
A dazed Dante and his Beatrice,
The wisteria, still pretending to die to its side,
That tsunami, still a hundred years away,
As we gathered together one afternoon,
Not thinking, then, that forty years later,
I would look over the walk,
Looking for that garden, my secret spot
Where I wished only to be by her side
Or just behind her tadpole hair,
for that one last college union photograph.

Nudes on the Beach

Wet to their pink tips the golden women
Sit staring at the tossing blue waves
Frothing spring foam; their fine wet
Symmetry slumped upon twinkling ilmenite
Under the lengthening shadows of the phallus
Rocks. Bright nipples glint like rose studs
As they sink them deeper into the crested sands
Among the shine of pebbles and colored dead shells.
Upon dumped footprints
The nudes breathe
Letting the bubbling foam rush quietly deep into
the deepening twilight zones of love.
They then gently rise,
Running down to the sea
Flaking away the tiny eels of water all over them,
As the dying sun strikes light
Upon the wet rosary of all the held back tears
Of our living and longing by the crying seas;
And holds them lit in dying orange hands awhile,
Upon the suddenly darkening waters.

The Painter of Evenings

Your young hands haul me up.
Together we climb the stairs,
And now as I stand upon the final step,
Goodbye has the quietness
Of distant waterfalls.

A small light limps across the hallway
Throwing away
Its crutches of shadows.
Here,
Silence curls its own tongue.

Gold mohurs in the park
Have suddenly turned dark.

To me,
And to my room.

Tablets in foil,
The Holy Book,
Beautiful sons far away,
Smiling from across their gold-rimmed frames.

In the corner,
The low catheter, the gift of a daughter,
Rubs shoulders with the clotted Crucifix.

And, I find a window here.
A window, magnificent as a Dali painting
Seamless into the near night
Where the calm painter of evenings

Gathers unto himself tethered lambs
That stare, and patiently await;

There, I take my place.

Digging

The soil I now pick
contains fragments of my dead.
They once saddened and happied themselves here
turning to sun and moon, quite puzzled,
then taking things as they came,
for granted. This hard brown laterite
I turn,
to plant a few periwinkles

stolen from the mound of one long obscure,
dead. They should grow well
here. So I turn out the millipedes curling up
ashamed of sudden expose,
into dark rings of topaz and sapphire.
Pinned to sudden light they have all coiled up
in abject surrender. These, I bury back
with the pushed out soil, strange roots crushing in,
lurking deep like soft nerve fibers
sending messages of thirst
to secret destinations. Each scoop of mud
brings more life to light,
lost like death underground,
doing odd jobs, ordained like saints salient
in dark recess
drawing salary in kind.
Mud-work is a kind of worship.
A silent thanksgiving, for a home, called earth.

Dash*

(The periwinkles upon us)

Now it is a time for dust
and bright wind flowers over us.
How beautiful they must grow,
the periwinkles all about
the crucifix upon you or me,
but must end up dying;
because like we did,
even here, we'll have love's
uncertain weather;
with no one to water us–
and perhaps a tourist will come
his camera hung upon his shoulder
and standing before us wonder
if he must shoot the young flowers upon you

Living Poetry

or all over me,
or just give up, after the reading
of the parenthesis,
comparing for himself
out of curiosity, about the dash in-between,
how long you lived, or I did,
after the first among us had left;
and then;
how perhaps we might have loved,
whether in life we were ever this close
as now together in our stones;
or will he really contemplate
of what you in your pride held back
all those years in that dash
when you could easily have given
the one who rode on your dream's horseback
right up to your wet lips wondering
how, ever, to get across
your bright red parted river;
but now it is over dash,
and we must forget,
the short hide seek we played,
and just know,
this is once again wind flower season,
there'll be bright periwinkles soon all over us again,
or perhaps, if the mud is not just right,
just the parenthesis of us naked, staring stone hard,
in the rain,
and the tourist crossing over
thinking to himself, no, there's no beauty,
nothing original in us for his frame,
and we let him pass, his feet over us,
his mind still jingling our parenthesis
his camera hung upon his shoulders
enjoying his vacation.

*Dash—The blank space between the years shown in parenthesis upon gravestones, denoting birth and death.

C. P. SURENDRAN

(1957–

C P Surendran was born in Palakkad, Kerala. He taught English literature at Calicut University before moving to Mumbai to work as a journalist. A selection of his poems was included in *Gemini II*. He thereafter published four collections of poems *Posthumous Poems, Canaries on the Moon, Portraits of the Space We Occupy* and *Available Light* (New and Collected Poems). His novels are *An Iron Harvest, Lost and Found, Hadal,* and *One Love and the Many Lives of Osip B.* Surendran was resident editor of The Times of India in Pune and senior editor with The Times of India in Delhi. He was chief editor, DNA. He lives in Delhi.

Living Poetry

A Note to the Self from Tranquebar

In a village by the noon, the sun rises in every room.
A shade of doubt, and I get the door. Vanakkam.
My father, brought to light by the sea. A petal I kept
To mark the pages of my life turns dark as the rum
Ove Gjedde took back to his silver mines in Kongsberg.
*

I try hard to add to the zero of my life without a sound.
In Tharangambadi, only the waves speak. Astride
A boat run aground, I watched the hot sea separate
Your thighs; from your crowned head, junk jewels of
        Janpath
Poured. Between breaths the earth keels over,
A million years to the minute. The sea.
The big, blue drawer of memory.
*

Where the long finger of water sleeps close to the sky,
A slow smoke of decay curls up like a dream.
Would that be a ghost ship drifting from Denmark to
        your hip?
Smoke meets wing. To an eagle, all that moves,
Moves towards its earth.
The Danes sold Dansborg Fort to the British,
Who, too, fled when the tide turned. Still the moon
        tugged
At the sea's heart. Still my father slaved through
        centuries of nights.
The beach flashes white and dark as the sea drags
        sunlight back.
*

At traffic lights, veiled women wail. Whips of blood
Split skin from songs. Drunks sight ships bulking
In empty air. Our ruins take shape as presidents
Wearing orange wigs. I uber; a cab my iPhone shook

Out of New York's brilliant dust; my head wrapped
In voices of David Bowie, Eminem,
The red-haired rest who overwhelm. The driver farts,
Hewn air, shaped like India, on the map. Shadows fall
Over the years, sunlight on soot. You eclipsed mirrors.
I made love to you every day after you swam away.

*

I see my father at the door, bright as a beam
Of butterflies. Ghosts flit, like wind on water,
Everywhere in broad daylight. On my shoulder,
His hand; muscled in care, brown. I've taken it nowhere
Out of town, though I've dragged my feet through the
    clouds of lead;
A moraine of sorts following my streets, like it was lost.
Where he touches burns, like a child on fire. When I
    arrive true,
The day before, or the day after, I must put my shoulder
    to the sea,
Watch it hiss; feel the waters part the heart like a
    passage to you.

Options for an Old Man in a Far Room

There are so many ways to end this, so what you see in
    the room lasts
For ever like the hill. What I see is a black couch, boat-
    shaped, kitsch,
Floating as the curtain lifts in the breeze over a table
    stacked with books,
And then sinking into its absence, the flying ocean
    returning unerringly
To land, the ships and fish on the magical lace,
    argonauts from untold
Voyages, at rest, as the curtain falls back in place
    between eternity and zilch.

I could go for a walk up the path winding through the
    scalloped hill,
A blue scoop of ice cream sliced by palms thin as lines
    drawn by knives,
A rock red in the sun like a cherry on top, step,
    casually, off the edge.
Or watch the cluck against the long-snouted rocks
    sunning
Like crocodiles, and run dry over the clouds toward the
    horizon
Where it all begins back again, thinking of Paul Celan in
    the Seine.
At night here, the moon is close and turns the water
    white.
Underfoot, the bridge rattles its bones to the passing
    cargoes of hearts.

Or read a line breathed out by the great, and marvel
    why the heart, after all
This, is yet fastened to the dying animal; how the
    reverse too, is true.
There is no curtain without a window, nothing flies
    that can't be moored.
It's the artifice looking for home in the blue. I am
    Argus of half a vessel.
A way to go would be to reach out for some such golden
    fleece as, say, Yeats
Wove and wore, which at my touch turned a shirt of
    flame, and charred clean
I fall, a wick of ash powdering the couch, the room
    empty as the sea, the books still.

House Hunting

I open the door with a key shaped like a dagger
And sharp enough to pick its way through
The ribs, unlock the phantom-hoard of the heart.

I cross the hall and find the floor tilting
Towards the kitchen smoking like a pipe
After supper, the bananas yellow, and hooked,
Hanging from the roof of their stalks.

The washroom tiles preserve in dust
Little footprints like memory's fossils.
The study in which I'd breathe my last
As I closed a book is shorter by a chapter.

The balcony creeps into a wall of vines
That come away in my hands as I fell
When I was eight, and the air echoes
My knee's screams when its cap cracked.

I push against a door
I'd missed off the hall
Bracing to see my father bent
Over the desk, a fat green pen
Lit between his fingers,
Writing up a storm.

And see a boy in shorts instead,
Watching ink flow along lines that glow.
He looks up and says, welcome home.

Back

I return by mirror to the same light
Playing with grime on the dull steelware
And the mothballs wasting away
In the witchery of their fumes, like a crime.
The kitchen has grown colder by a lightyear. A polite
Place for poltergeist and blight.

The fan still spins in the spoon, though.
I am grateful for this comfort. But the stove
Doesn't light and the tap refuses to turn.
Stealth stifles the air; the house conspires.

Home, I tell the man turning away in the mirror.
My captive. Let him go?
Cut my wrist and set off a little sunset.
Let him go.

Signature

Gestures I trace to my mother
Her hands pick their aerial way
Through dire states of mind
The agonies of taking care
Of children who returned prodigally
From vocations. Her fingers
Are in curlers; they roll, preen
And part the air, knead a word
Into an abandon of tears. Forever
In motion, her hands have no limits
Nor remember the courtesy knock
Before a door is opened. Free hands
Lying farthest from gravity
Into high theatre where all words bow down
To the strung soliloquy of gestures

And the oracular act of nerves. Hands
That discern disasters balling up
Like storm clouds horizons away;
Whose certain coming she lets you know
By conjuring from sideboards
A crushed trail of broken glass.
Like the mute, my mother counts
The sinners and the saints of the house
On her fingertips, the air around her
Bruised by signs of love.

Two

You shift in bed, next to me,
Your voice just right
For weather reports, blight.

'These are the words you like,
Dark, descend, stairs, nude, lantern, death
And you believe this is what your life is,
A few words, but perhaps not in that order.
Everything is richer than you think.'

I believe you are right.
Each life prints
Its dictionary;
Some a thesaurus
Of just one word.
What's yours?

I keep my peace
Aware of the sheath
Of space between us
Just right for a sword to hide
And worry why it takes
Just two people for such quiet.

Reflection

There was the sight when I caught a bus late one night
Of a man driving a pin up the heel of a baby bawling
In the arms of his mother. I got out with him
At Harbor Terminus where trips turned around.

What makes you do that, I asked?

Oh, my friend, he said, I train spoilt babies
To grow up tough, so they take the world
In their stride, and hopes of the mothers
Are not belied. I'm sure you took your first steps
On shattered glass. It shows. Be my guest,
Come and have a drink at home.

Some other time, I said, and I was afraid
It might all turn out to be wrong.

He smiled: I, too, took my time
To find my trade. Come again, same bus,
And let's set it right; at night we see it all
In a different light.

On the far sea I saw a ship docked
Between two stars, shedding and loading
Its cargo of fireflies. From darkened homes
I heard babies wailing through the night.

Sparrows

In Gaza, Kobane, Kashmir
There is a moment of hush,
In retrospect,
Before a bomb explodes
And the air begins to bleed.

This is the time no clock marks
Because hearts are about to stop.

When it goes off, sound and light
Separate, like a sieve, mother and child;
Human innards trail on the road,
And festoon the branches
Like badges pinned to military green.
The clamours of those yet breathing
Mingle with screams out of sight;
Nightmares haul the after them
And the high-voltage evening rusts
And sparkles along the razor wires.

Some will gather their last breath
To ask what happened to passers-by.
Others will think of their children
Left to wander the earth looking
For what they lost
Till they met death eye to eye.
And, cruelly, no one remembers the enemy,
Or whose turn it's next; from whose chest
Flesh will fly like sparrows from a nest.

Harbinger

Work the last breath to a loaf of bread.
The axes and spades synchronized, heave
And push. Last night it rained.
From the well of the day
We drew blood.
Each night we come and go
Carrying in our eyes
A little bit of those
Who left behind their jackets
On the hooks.

Into the unknown
They carry their numbers
Which weigh more than the earth.
Shoes, glasses, gods survive
Us. These things
We fear for our children.
Their fingers curl
Like worms around hope.
We step in through a door.
Nothing comes back.
Here we were, in the woods
Far from the earth and echoes.

*

I have arrived alone
Dreaming of this rented room
With a tap,
Close to the tracks.
I can hear the trains brake
And rend
At the unutterable stations
Tending to the journeys' end,
My hands wet with rain
From forbidden lands.

Prospect

While you were looking away
A dog yawned in the sun
And in the distance
A train blindfolded
By a tunnel
Window by window
Regained vision.

I thought of all the things
That could happen
When we are looking away

The universe we miss in a blink.

From Catafalque

'I go as the first, at the head of many (who still have to die) I go in the midst of many (who are now dying). What will be the work of Yama (the ruler of the departed) which today has to do unto me?'— Nachiketa to his father in Katha-Upanishad who in a fit of anger gifted him to Yama the Ruler of the Dead.

Post Natal

A room secreting smells
Laundered linen
Breathing out camphor.
Old Spice, old books, soap ghosting
Air with scent of rose.
Blue ink gleaming thick in vat of glass,
On the roll-top desk, the fat green pen on its side, run
    dry and smoking
Where it stopped. Lunar blips gilding the corner basin
    of water.
The floor waxed black verging on the brink
Of light, a dark pond mirroring the advance of the
    night.
Wet whiff of a body wasting.

My father on the cot in white, straight as a corpse in a
    coffin.
The hours crawl about him in ambush

Detonating memory cells at each intractable breath
Burning synapses down like a bridge
Weighting his tongue down
With speech slush.
Between flashes he wakes up blind, shakes a hand at
          the carnage
Laying him bare to the crib. Remembers neither the
          revolt
Of the beginnings, nor the submission at arrival.
          Between birth
And death, there's nothing. Not even sorrow.
My father is a big baby, born today, gone tomorrow.

Threshold

The roses are on their own.
The grass spreads
Like water from an upturned urn.
Between mornings smudged blue like bruises
And evenings bubbling like blood
Along the broken arteries of the sky
The road narrowing through hedgerows,
Hens, fallow fields, darkening stream
Slows towards home to halt
At my father's feet, far from town.
He clasps his hand over his head,
The softening crown.
And I see
His hands are no longer hard or brown.

Rout

At first, you did not let on
Bent over the rampart of your desk, an old king
        surveying
What's left, the sunlight flagging white the paper
On which you were surrendering, face close
To the fabled pen, the last of the language you lived by
Writer redivivus, inhaling ink, memory's blue blood.
I look over your shoulder at the random craft
Practicing on you its witchery
And see with eyes that praised the kingdom
You set up once with your phrases
Mutant shapes, in singles and droves, freak alphabet
O forgetfulness, while your hands shake in time's
        fetters.

Permanent Revolution

April now in the Kremlin, machines part
Late snow on either side, soft white hair falling
Away to reveal the black scalp of the road.

The wall of the Square
And all that's red when it was bright
Congeals like clotted blood into the night;
Everything except the snow.

Here in April, the eviscerated earth
Awaiting your arrivals rolls down
A carpet of cracks. You are the filling in the blanks.
In the tonsuring solar fire of the South,
Leaves curl like smoke.
Flame of the forest is a Franciscan Friar.
Only the bougainvillea rouses the rabble-air
With its speech of blood.

If this your summer, do you give a damn?
Speak. Do you, sir, remember
All that you said in praise of the USSR?
Of the Kremlin, Lenin, Red Star?
The thirty books you wrote, now footnotes
To a history that was false? How see now
Your passion for that which was not?
The faith no God could shake?

Such illusions that make us brave
We carry to the grave.
Go down, and still find rest
In the shade of the red flag
Follow the shining star
To worlds revolving beyond summer and snow
Assured, in Moscow, embalmed Lenin sleeps
Dead as you, and dressed to kill again the Czar.

I

I who hid my face in the wear you left
In the basket for wash, Cuticura
Mixed with sweat, Old Spice, Brylcreem
On the side, so your casket of odours
Would bear me through the night's dark tides.

I who went around the ancient house papering
Over cracks through which lizards of light
Crept, and closing windows so I was free
For a while longer from the gaze of those
Who slept, except you who asked what it was
With me about light, and I said, I was afraid
Of others awaking too early in my world.
Now, as I stretch myself to dim your lamp
And close the window on the other side,

I you asked me
What it was about the light
As when I was in the first grade
The answer still is, I am afraid.

Post Crypt

The letter you wrote when you were thirteen
Expressing concern for your father's health
His foundering fortune
One hand on orphaned heart, the other pushing
The early pen, that he may yet find,
In his paternal reserve, enough to draw for ink
And paper, a fresh lease,
So you may continue your studies, please,
Has reached me this morning, seventy years later
While shifting your books and such closed chapters
Including the one on the boy who dropped out of
        school.

I'd like to tell you: I'm in a position now
To honour your request that cast a shadow
On your father's face and raised his brow.

Homage to a Hen

Once upon a time, at first light, you set out to the post
        office
To mail a report which you did with a satisfaction
That conjured up from a sidewalk café, fried eggs,
        sunny side up
Fluffy as a cloud on a day in spring. I can still feel the
        buds
That bloomed on my tongue, and I never

Had a breakfast like that since, which made me sing.
If that day was an empire, I was king.

Today I was up at dawn
To tell you that a hen that laid such timeless eggs
Deserved a hug, but was brought short
At your door
Behind which you lay wholly beyond recall.

Dog

The last time I saw you happy
You had lost your way on a visit
To the city, and as the morning
Mourned into noon, you returned home
Tired as a dog back from woods,
With a stranger at heel, who said,
No, not to mention, it was part of the game
He too had a father like mine,
But put a collar on him, he said, a name
And an address, so people know
Where he comes from, where to go.

That's all I needed, my father said,
Rolling over, tongue out, playing dead.

Boy

The great man you wanted me to become,
The world's best surgeon or some such,
A success story that suffered no disgrace,
Brought his father pride,
At this late hour come back making light
Of the promises not made good.

Here I am finally,
Short, bearded, bald; a veined hand
Pinned under a tattooed cross
Placating in vain the heart's swell
At your ride turning in, the other
Holding yours, wishing you well.

Translation

Shadows drift under the street lamps,
Merge and pass. If it were thus, pared of flesh
And bone, what matters it who heads the batch,
Who at the centre, marching towards Yama?
You showed me the earth. Now each difficult breath
You draw weighs me down with what you gave.
I am in debt to all I see and hear, paddy glittering
Green in the field of day, the stream plucking its way
Through stars, the moon caught in flight in a throng
Of thorns. Your gifts are at work even after death.

Time effects its slow translation of the original
Into elements, the living text's various versions.
I must bow down to the ground I tread,
Recall with grace what's lost as you pass
Into the earth and air, holy as the Host in bread.

JEET THAYIL

(1959-

Jeet Thayil was born in Mamalasserie, Ernakulam, Kerala. His book of poems *These Errors Are Correct* won the Sahitya Akademi award for poetry. His novel *Narcopolis*, was a close contender for the Booker Prize, and it won him the DSC Prize. Jeet Thayil edited *The Bloodaxe Book of Contemporary Indian Poets*. He wrote the libretto for *Babur in London* which toured Switzerland and the U.K. His novels include *Low* and *Names of the Women*. He is a visiting professor of poetry at the University of Goa. Jeet Thayil is also a musician. He lives in Bangalore.

Living Poetry

Self-Portrait

Unhappiness is a kind of yoga, he tells himself
each morning, a breath meditation; besides,
do you want to be happy or do you want to write?
When he lifts saucepan to stove, images atone
forever in his hands. Ghosts of celebrations past
throw themselves lemming-like into the meagre
flame, each small act attended by a host of demons,
friendly and not. The world is code, smoke signals the
dead have left us to decipher, knowing we cannot.
At nightfall, exhausted by toil, he falls deep into the
dreamless light changes, the dead or dying sea.
A mountain moves and nobody notices. The world
is old and set in its ways, and K. is saying, Of course
There's hope, there's always hope, but not for us.

Future Watercolour

The black cars huddle on the street and
settle in for the night.

One day we'll leave this place. The cars
will trumpet after us.

Goodbye, beasts, street. Goodbye, me, you.
Hello, new ruin.

What then? Years later in Berlin, you will
Return as the wounded

flesh of a pear on my bedside table.

Separation's Sonnet

What are you doing, what improvised thing?
In a borrowed room your cell phone rings,
each ring measures the floor, the rungs
of your dream. Holding, I ask how you sing,
and for whom. To imagine the bed you're in,
the vertiginous smile that will break him,
the man whose roses bleed at your window.
To want is to wait, as I do in the place I know,
my breathing loud and single as the room,
its smell of spider dust and old perfume.
Each small thing lasts longer than the shiver
that is life. I fix the remembered instant:
you on your feet, singing, shaking a river
of salt from our shared overheating skin.

Boyhood

All are agreed he was sly about his needs.
When the daily ordeal of prayer was done,
he went on: his prayers had just begun.
But when his father stepped out,
the boy took the book and posed with it
in the mirror above the sink, his eyebrows
knotted into one. His soul, some said, yearned
to sink into a bowl of ecumenical blood.
What he dreaded were holidays and weekends,
his father home, the house silent. He dreamed of
flight, of silver-bodied Boeings that sailed the
skies like battleships, silent beings from
elsewhere, he at the controls, silent too, raining
cotton candy on the stupefied. Undecided
about God—who he is, what he wants—he knew
fear, not love. He wanted obedience, not choice.
More than the blood he drew from the

neighbourhood's cats—each lasting longer
than the one before, injured where no one saw—
he loved the servants who cleaned and
cooked, loved the smell, the hawk and spit,
the blasphemy of it. When the old cook
washed himself in the servants' bathroom,
he'd wait outside for the man to appear
in a towel. Cleansed, he breathed the deep
odour of carbolic sweat and Dettol.
He loved disorder, the chaos of rain pounding
on the town, the flooded roads. At thirteen,
his father prone in the back of the ambulance,
his mother wild, he let panic thrill and encircle him.
He heard cartoon voices in the next room
and trained himself not to move, trained his
eyes in the mirror to be flat, to withhold news.
At the beach he sat away from his relatives.
When children's voices echoed from the water,
the water whose genius trembled in the sun,
he heard not children, but the cries of the doomed,
and lifting his head saw men women babies,
bodies aloft, lifting downward like
butterflies from the towers of the world.

53 Views of Abstraction, 1 Rhyme, 0 Blackbirds

1. In a red and blue swatch of sky
2. The only moving thing was I,
3. And a kite of three minds.
4. One was made of fire,
5. One of ice,
6. The third mind was made of cumuli.
7. A spun metal kite
8. Made ON 5/6/78 (not 79)
9. Was no small part of the pantomime;
10. It was the play entire.

11. In a map of the high
12. World, Osip, the only clear sign
13. Was the fat unshy
14. Cockroach on Stalin's smile.
15. I ask, Why?
16. You reply,
17. The lords will tire
18. Of misrule. We must bide
19. Our time.
20. The dish, of Parsi Spiced
21. Stir-Fried
22. Squid, serves 4 or 5.
23. I do not know which to desire,
24. The red name or, aiie,
25. The blue. Aye,
26. Or the yellow room where names are cried.
27. The interlocking tri-
28. Angle and two tied
29. Circles are one. The woman is a find.
30. I don't care how much, she's mine.
31. She points to the sun, which shines
32. In red and yellow smears, in lines
33. Of fine
34. Yellow and red, and indigo dye
35. That fills my
36. Line of sight.
37. Are these specks or birds that fly
38. In formation, a crazy Y?
39. O Vengeful, thy
40. Eyes are dry.
41. Thou leavest us with a sign
42. And a question, Which is nigh:
43. The beauty of the succubi
44. Or the beauty of the lie?
45. Thou, as wise
46. One, or as love Crucified?
47. Hi,

48. Shakti, it's New Year's Eve, 2007, 5.49
49. p.m. We're in a coffee shop in Manali and I'm
50. Looking at the ice
51. On the Himalayas and writing this line.
52. I have no idea at the time
53. But in three months to the day you will die.

The Heroin Sestina

What was the point of it? The stoned
life, the chased, snorted, shot life. Some low
comedy with a cast of strangers. Time
squashed flat. The 1001 names of heroin
chewed like language. Nothing now to know
or remember but the dirty taste

of it, and the names: snuff, Death, a little taste,
H—pronounce it etch –, sugar, brownstone,
scag, the SHIT, ghoda gaadi, 4 china, You-Know,
garad, god, the gear, junk, monkey blow,
the law, the habit, the material, cheez, heroin.
The point? It was the wasted time,

which comes back lovely sometimes,
a ghost sense say, say that hard ache taste
back in your throat, the warm heroin
drip, the hit, the rush, the whack, the stone.
You want it now, the way it lays you low,
flattens everything you know

to a thin white line. I'm saying, I know
the pull of it: the skull rings time
so beautiful, so low
you barely hear it. Itch this blind toad taste.
When you said, 'I mean it, we live like stones,'
you broke something in me only heroin

could fix. The thick sweet amaze of heroin,
helpless its love, its know-
ledge of the infinite. Why push the stone
back up the hill? Why not leave it with the time-
keep, asleep at the bar? Try a little taste
of something sweet that a sweet child will adore, low
in the hips where the aches all go. Allow
me in this one time and I'll give you heroin,
just a taste
to replace the useless stuff you know.
Some say it comes back, the time,
to punish you with the time you killed, leave you stone

sober, unknowing, the happiness chemical blown
from your system, unable to taste the word heroin
without wanting its stone one last time.

Trout Fishing at Night

'Mom!' the boy yells, running into the kitchen.
'I was standing at the window and a man waved
his fish at me.' Breathing hard, tugging at
his mother's hand, he wills her to come and see,
his eyes bright with unshed tears. She wonders
at the pitch of his voice, hysteria unbroken,
and rues his world's commonplace disasters.
She lets him lead her back. Mother and son
stand by the open window in the dark.
In the house across the way, in a yellow
square of kitchen light, a shirtless man
stalks the floor, hair plastered down his head,
animated in conversation with himself.
When he stops directly in front of them,
As if he knows they're there, she clutches the boy.
A silvery trout dangles from the man's fly.

Fixing Father

It's time I made my peace with you, father,
soon I'll go stupid from this sly disease,
I'll be wetting myself soon, stretched out here,
begging for the swift resolution of steel.
To know you shall outlive me after all,
what a bitterness that once used to be.
Every exertion I made for a bed,
for bread or for wine, undermined by this:

never, but never, to aspire for greatness.
I remember the hot sand burning,
a hundred fingers of sand in my eyes,
hot breath of sand singing in the desert,
everywhere, anywhere the cruelties of sand,
and never calling, not aloud, for you.
I had a pride as implacable as yours,
useless to me now on this wooden perch

paying so dearly for sins never mine.
I am begging now of strangers, of fools,
charlatans all in their medicine robes
and others with butchers' hands, of women
who weep and wail at will it seems, of you.
I beg now of you, father, I forgive
these tireless eruptions of the flesh.
Even in death I do your will.

Pushkin Knew Heaven

(A Place Where Nothing Happens)

The first hint of first light
brings me instantly awake.

You stir gently in your sleep,
dig yourself deeper into bed,
my pillow over your head.

The newspaper at the door is cold
from its journey across the city. I
make coffee, as I do each morning,
scan the headlines, sip from the cup,
look out at the quiet street.

There it is, all of it, and it's nothing
short of a miracle.

If there is such a thing as happiness,
it is this.

Apocalypso

North American angels die young,
cheeks hollow from blowing out forest
fires, marks of past beauty still
visible on earlobe, nipple, bicep, nostril,
skinny always, bearded sometimes, haunted by
waking dreams of the Mall of All America.
Tiny spoons or half-razors dangling
from neck chains, American angels live
alone with their pets.

Rosy-cheeked, skulls shaved to the skin,
beery border-line booze-hounds,
British angels are strictly segregated,
not by gender but colour and accent,
white is wary of brown, brown of black,
black of yellow, yellow of white, and so,
perfectly, on. They will deny to the end
that they're racist, past it, pissed. The talk is

of the good old days. Only sunshine can
reduce them to silence.

Angels in Spain are endangered, the few that
remain are transfixed in the glare of meat—
packed freezer trucks pounding the highway to
Madrid or Toledo. Spanish angels love to
eat and drink and spend their inheritance wisely.
In France, the angels live only in Paris,
or are headed there, or come from there; are wary
of the rain, for they know French rain can kill;
do not die of tuberculosis; see no value
in misery, poetry or poverty. Absinthe they
can take or leave.

Slavery binds Asian angels in a new impoverished
brotherhood, gaunt angels, permanently deferred,
who speak, dream, write and kill English,
language of their once and future masters. Life
is good as long as there's television and tourism,
and if there isn't, well, then, life can be altered
organically, chemically, life can be recycled,
and home wired to the dish that cannot feed.
Dona Paulita, meanwhile, caresses the bundle
wriggling her arms: Pierre, the pink and sacred
baby pig squealing to be fed. Asian
angels go hungry.

Imaginary Homecoming

At river's edge
I cup my hands,
drink until I'm drunk,

the cool water
made sweeter

with knowledge.

This is the end
of wandering under
other skies,

the untrue north of exile.
How many camps
like this one?

Heat or cold,
or a promise of better;
we washed our thirst

with more thirst,
ready always
for weather.

Each day
brought its measure
of movement.

Cow-dung houses
abandoned, cook fires
doused, horses slaughtered.

So many rude tongues
become familiar,
we learned to keep

our own language
secret and true
to our ears.

The rank rubric
of memory,
our only constant,

and the women,
children,
exhaustion.

I let the water
wet my face, taste
spiced sun on my tongue,

woodsmoke
from the houses
on the hill.

Yet Another Mother Poem

Light careens
through my veins,
makes me whole,
I inhabit

uninhabitable days.
Small whips of rain
crack at my back,
make me holy.

Water and air
pump red squalls
of love or pain.
I fall

into your room
on frayed flat heels,
pillbox hat flat,
hands of opium tincture.

My winter breath blows

small sacraments
of air. There,
then gone.

For Agha Shahid Ali

Who among us will escape the hand of water?
No check, no eye is dry in the land of water.

Bolt tight the windows, the wind is fierce tonight.
Read the collected works, unsigned, of water.

Tomorrow, my love, we'll walk our bereaved city.
We'll see what the streets understand of water.

Last night the moon said your love would abide.
How wet are your eyes with the brand of water!

Someone is singing a widower's song in Malayalam.
I'm reaching for your hair, beribboned, of water.

When the starlings return to the streets of Manhattan,
Wake me. Till then am I a man, unmanned, of water.

In the Almanac of Rain you will find all my lines,
Each rhyme and refrain, each ampersand of water.

Jeet, meet Shahid, your guide to the future.
He'll teach you to play a baby grand of water.

Jeet Thayil

New Year, Goa

The midnight's cataracts whiten,
and here's the sea hissing
its one stuttered consonant.

Leaf-printed, you track the moon
to a beached, bearded hull, a room
of vertigo or freedom

that narrows like memory.
Small flames ascend a tree
of light. The two-and-thirty

palaces of Bodhisattvam
tremble on the vellum-
smooth water, like flotsam.

If tonight the mind is queasy,
drawing thoughts like flies, he
is fine too with every crazy

scheme you devise, none crazier
than this pilgrimage to a pier
that seems to have disappeared,

leaving you seaborne at last,
ahead of you the past,
and all its famous cities lost.

Malayalam's Ghazal

Listen! Someone's saying a prayer in Malayalam.
He says there's no word for 'despair' in Malayalam.

Sometimes at daybreak you sing a Gujarati garba.

At night you open your hair in Malayalam.

To understand symmetry, understand Kerala.
The longest palindrome is there, in Malayalam.

When you've been too long in the rooms of English,
Open your windows to the fresh air of Malayalam.

Visitors are welcome in The School of Lost Tongues.
Someone's endowed a high chair in Malayalam.

I greet you my ancestors, O scholars and linguists.
My father who recites Baudelaire in Malayalam.

Jeet, such drama with the scraps you know.
Write a couplet, if you dare, in Malayalam.

Letter from a Mughal Emperor, 2006

Nothing here's worth a tick.

I hid everything except the heads. They respect
　　　　slaughter.

They respect only slaughter. They forget the other
　　　　things we
brought them, the ghazals, the gardens, the rice and
　　　　symmetry.

It's an affliction to grow up motherless, with your lady
　　　　mother
living beside you.

They have many images, but they have no God. They're
　　　　fit only
for war.

Even the dogs are second rate.

In Tashkent I had no money, no country or hope of one,
          only
humiliation. But among the people I found much
          beauty. No
pears are better.

There are no accidents. There's only God.

Tending to his doves on the eve of battle, my father
          flew into
ravine at the fortress of Akhsi.

He became a falcon. I became emperor.

Sometimes, when I eat a Kabul melon, I remember my
          father
and you.

I've forgotten more than I've seen, but I haven't
          forgotten enough.

There's only one way to live in a place like this, with
          your
disgust close at hand.

One night I took majoun because the moon was
          shining. The
next day I took some more, at sunrise.

I enjoyed wonderful fields of flowers, flowers on all
          sides. I saw
an apple sapling with five or six leaves placed regularly
          on each
branch.

No painter could have done this.

I made a schedule. Saturday, Sunday, Tuesday and
 Wednesday for
wine, the other days for majoun.

Your letter puzzled me:

*The people are caught between constant spiritual anguish and
 a faith that
will give meaning to the question that consumes them: the
 dual substance
of Krishna, the yearning of man to know God. Between the
 spirit and
the flesh, a great unwinnable war.*

Dear friend, write clearly, with plain words. Writing
 badly will
make you ill.

Once, in an orchard, I was sick with fever and vision. I
 was
young, but I prepared myself.

A hundred years or a day, in the end you'll leave this
 place.

Long ago, my grandfather's face looked into mine, I
 think with
love.

Now when we speak it's of ghazals, of metrics and
 rhyme or of
our most famous massacres.

When he conquered Lahore he planted a banana tree. It
 thrived,
even in that climate.

His memory is so good it gives him a second life. Mine
 gives
only a partial one.

It's no more than I need.

My Lie

If you marry me
I'll give you this poem
in which a ship full of men,
hoarse from drinking,
pull themselves through a sea
boiling with rain.
It's an epic poem
on which I've been
working
so long my eyes have dimmed.
It's yours if you marry me.

Where This One Came From

1

Tonight she walks in moonlight,
reaching for something she cannot name,
a twist of muscle maybe, maybe a knot inside.

She will not promenade tonight,
she will skulk beside you if you're lucky.
(Skulk is a word stolen from the future.)

She's a sober as fuck, no? No, not as fuck,
sober as stone cold jelly, staring for a face,
her own, in the eyes of johns and jimmies.

(I think I meant jaans and jaanus,
considering which side of the hemisphere.)
'Vampire junkie from hell,' private joke

she's too distracted to note.
She finds a cheap hotel, vestibule
lit by a single yellow bulb.

2

On the bed, she spreads her need
open like a pack of cards.
You take your pick, but it's wrong, homes.

She examines the four-chambered room,
the heart & comes to a slow decision:
the penthouse. Pay letter/never.

She opens wide legs & arms,
gives herself completely, comes
in the sick blue colours of withdrawal.

Poem is as poem does & is done by.
Now watch poem sleep the pure slumber
of children, drunks, fools. By first light

she will vanish, leaving you, shadow.

Jeet Thayil

My Grandmother's Funeral

What stories you know, closed in the worm's dominion,
composed for the doomed enclosure of bone,
hair and fingernail fragment; the yellow hoops removed
from your ears and wrists. *I alone am left to tell this love.*
Light drowns in water, unseen from this church,
whitewashed on a hill in the lush south. *I alone am left.*
The congregation stands entranced, white shirts and
        mundus
starched, sung aloft on ancient rhythms, talismanic
        glow
of hymns repeated in a tongue all of us remember and
        nobody
understands. Some words promise an impossible
        redemption:
barachimo, deyvam, shudham, slomo. *My words are*
        water.
The evening censers pass scent of smoke
from hand to hand, from end to end of a sunlit room
where Syriac, the first figure of faith, waits with his
        fierce
accountings—your ally in the conundrums of Christ,
his mother, the red heart bared. *Here am I, empty of*
        words.
At dawn, in single beds, you and your husband lay
        chaste
in matrimony, a wedlock holy as hands, *I am made mute,*
perfected your children, the young dead become legend,
oversaw strict enunciation of shekels, rice and prayer.
The slow erosions of memory, tidy acres overgrown,
ungentle stripping of faces, names, ignoble disrobing
for the writer you were, grace, the first of our long line.
Crawling to eternity, alone in the one house so many
        sons
and daughters embarked from, *left alone to die,* you faced
the curse of longevity placed on the women of our tribe

with a wilful retrieval of dignity: the clenched refusals
of food and water, final naysaying to the sanctification
of all who lived to your great age: a life-affirming *No!*
that resounds now from the walls, fallen, of your house.

Wedding Picture

Late at night, by my side,
You are the loneliest ranger.
Dreams wormhole the future,
Show you how to stop this life.

Birds drop, skies lighten.
Round the cape of no hope
We awake, you wife, I husband
Our ship a room of wet hope.

Some mornings, the moon holds
The wall like a slim white lizard.
Your fingers read the world's
Book of Hours, backward.

Bees stop, flowers die,
Grief takes its human shape.
These are the signs we make
To know we are alive

.

VIJAY NAMBISAN

(1963-2017)

Vijay Nambisan had his ancestral home in Thayoor village in Erumappetty, Thrissur, Kerala. He was born in Neyveli, Tamil nadu. Viay won the first All India British Council Poetry Competition (Poetry Society, India and the British Council). He made his debut with *Gemini*, an edition he shared with Jeet Thayil. Vijay's first collection of poems was *First Infirmities.* In between, he published *Two Measures of Bhakthi* (Translations of the poetry of Poontanam and Melpathur Narayana Bhattathiri), and two books of non-fiction on rural, societal issues close to his heart. Vijay Nambisan was married to the doctor-novelist Kavery Nambisan. His Collected poems *These Were my Homes* appeared posthumously in 2018.

The Miracle of the Pomegranate

In the August rain the flowers are changing
The shape of the tree. It was light and airy,
Holding its colours high above the earth, arranging
For itself a crown with sure fingers. Now rudely laden
With miracles, it regards the wetness below.

Fruits swell in crimson and yellow, strange
To pluck from grey air. Is there nothing else to do
But life must poke its secrets up through the shoots,
Up past the leaves and into the flowers,
Filling them slowly as if trying on gloves;

Nothing to do but after the merest shower
It should be thrusting earth aside with green plumes
Simply to put the tree in proper perspective—
Unwanted things coming again and again to birth,
Ignoring the fact that the gardener's due tomorrow.

He'll mutter to himself, Nothing useless nothing
                wasted,
But the tree's grown so tall that half its prizes
Will only come to the wasteful bats and thieving
Squirrels, then be left to lose their colours, rotting,
Laying the secret bare to be sympathized with.

Madras Central

The black train pulls in at the platform,
Hissing into silence like hot steel in water.
Tell the porters not to be so precipitate—
It is good, after a desperate journey,

To rest a moment with your perils upon you.

The long rails recline into a distance
Where tomorrow will come before I know it.
I cannot be in two places at once:
That is axiomatic. Come, we will go and drink
A filthy cup of tea in a filthy restaurant.

It is difficult to relax. But my head spins
Slower and slower as the journey recedes.
I do not think I shall smoke a cigarette now.
Time enough for that. Let me make sure first
For the hundredth time, that everything's complete.

My wallet's in my pocket; the white nylon bag
With the papers safe in its lining—fine;
The book and my notes are in the outside pocket;
The brown case is here with all its straps secure.
I have everything I began the journey with,

And also a memory of my setting out
When I was confused, so confused. Terrifying
To think we have such power to alter our states,
Order comings and goings: know where we're not
             wanted
And carry our unwantedness somewhere else.

Cats Have No Language

Cats have no language to tell their world.
The moon is a midsummer madness
That satisfies foolish chroniclers;
But their paws gloat on the captured mouse
—The slither beneath the stair—the silent bat
That drifted on a moonbeam into the house
Gashed a slitted eye into a flicker

And was gone. The moon is too much for the cat.

The light is too much for cats: that is why
At the human snarl behind the torch
The keen eyes turn slate, and a careless slouch
Replaces the studied artistry, frozen flash
Before the kill. They do not like the light
But have no language save the curving slash
And the sideways sculpture at a whisker's touch
Cats are dumb when they walk in the night.

Cats are clever at night, but the sun
Melts the moon's glitter out of their eyes,
Leaves them children's toys and the green trees.
Now how can fingers soothe the shoulder-knots,
Trust the silken purr, the kind eyes? Cat,
I know, I have seen her sleeping thoughts
Tense and stalk savagely in the night's peace.
But cats need no language to do all that.

The Attic

There is too much rubbish in the attic,
Unni, would you go up and see
What's worth keeping?

Grandmother, the temple doves are nesting there
And the floor is sifted with soft down.
The sills are occupied with their lovemaking,
And their throaty burbles fill the room with sound.

Unni, the doves have nested there for centuries,
But would you see what the attic holds?

Grandmother, bats hang from the rafters
And the corners reek of their peculiar smell.

One flew past my head suddenly,
Swerving away as if he didn't like it.
Grandmother, what makes them fly like that?

She sighs. Unni, the bats have flown there
Since I was a child, and for all I know
They are the same bats still. They always fly like that.
But what valuables are there in the attic?

Unni leaves hesitantly, and it is a long time
Before his footsteps sound the stairs again.
She waits, relieved.
        Grandmother, I am sorry,
But I found this piece of carved wood in the corner
By the teak chest, and was looking at it all this time.
Isn't it very pretty? Who made it? Can I keep it?

        She is silent for a long while,
Her fingers groping for the secrets in the grain,
Her mind for words and faces.
And then she says, You may go out and play now, dear
        Unni.
I see there's much that is valuable in the attic.

She waits to hear his delighted shouts
In the courtyard by the well, then with slow
Time-burdened steps, feeling within herself
Every moment she has lived, acknowledging tiredly
Every wrinkle in her breasts, she begins to climb.

Grandfather's Beard

They call it grandfather's beard,
This windblown seed with white filaments:
I never saw such a beard on my grandfather,
But this feathery manifestation of air,

This oak heart holding the world to itself
And sending the winds to be so diffused,
It has something of the look in my grandfather's eye—
There were people, he said, unaffected by him
And there were those by whom he was not affected—
So also this secret (that I cannot associate
With any green plant clutching earth with its roots,
But seems to me rather the tangible form of a kiss,
Such a kiss as I would want to touch with my lips)
Floats on the light wind, and if you see it
It is there, and if you don't happen to
You are just as well off.
            I would like my poem to be
Like my grandfather's beard, to be airy
In the lean wind, to look up at the clouds
And laugh. There are people unaffected
By poetry, and there are those whom poetry
Disregards—I would like to write a poem
Like grandfather's beard.

Poetic Licence

When my grandfather grew to be an old man,
he was a little mad:
        his hair turned black again
and his voice held its own, and his eyes
asked incessantly for answer, an answer.

My mother would frown,
and shake her head, and laugh;
but she would hold him, would roll his paan
and wipe his mouth.
            And later,
sitting by herself in the dusk,
she would be sad awhile.

For my grandfather was once a poet
and some of the world's weight
had lain upon his shoulders.

After Six Drinks

I am grieving for everything which has occurred
To put me where I am, and us where we are—
I am sorrowing even for what holds us—in a word,
For everything I am grieving without bar.

I am grieving for my friends who are laughing now,
Let them. My heart is filling so much it cannot speak.
Now they are laughing, see only tomorrow how
They will cry to God. But of course, the gods are Greek

And they find it so funny, our small disaster.
          Someone was whispering that hearts are meant to break—
I am willing my heart to beat faster and faster,
Finishing life quickly. This is no ordinary ache.
I am pouring my sorrow into a little cup,
Just to drown the gods in—a libation, nothing more,
And when we are being happy and the roof is on the
          floor
Someone can reach out and casually drink me up.

Holy, Holy

The rain threatens this ordinary day
With magic. Things that grow manifest,
Plainly, the unnatural: more sure
And permanent is the unwalked way,
Lifeless air, stone unencumbered

With feelings; not obsessed, therefore pure.

Yet even metal has a life that cries
For use, even crystals ask to be touched—
How much weaker are these green and clinging loves,
These hollow souls that populate the skies
With what they aspire to. Reality
In itself is content, and needs no proofs.

When I was young enough to treat these things
Without consciousness, I could cast my mind
Into that emptiness whereof all is made
And ask, without my imaginings,
What is?
    Nothing answered nothing, and in that space
I knew myself unliving, unafraid.

Narcissus in the Drought

Watch thirstily the dry hollows etched sharp in the sun,
The tortured lives reconciled to death, until
The craving will suffice, and remembered waters fill
The long naked channels, gurgling run
Or shimmer like mirages in exhausted eyes.

Wait, wait in the heat, stale air and aching heat,
Wait among the stifled shapes and attempt to keep
In vanished rivers drowned, or beneath the earth and
    deep,
A memory of peace; beneath six feet
Of dying rock, in a cool, dank hollow underground.

Here there is no relief—this changelessness is worst—
But one thin ghost of shadow at which I ever stare:
Dry and faint as dust, it seems with me to share
A need for more than water, a thirst

That water cannot assuage, but water must.

I will the flickering image to move towards the shore:
There is no stream; but my memory will flow
Always along its course. Though remembrance is slow
And not enough, yet ever more and more
The stream sounds in my ears,
                     with a voice both clear and hoarse.
There is flood in the air; in the mouth, great thirst,
A prayer to the shadow to move a little more
Towards a vision I know possessed me there before.
I cannot hope to live now; but first
It must hurt somewhat, to perish, not knowing why.

Ducks

They hammered in the stakes and wound the long nets round,
Blue nets of nylon, about as high as where
They wound their dhotis, and I wondered as
I sat by the raining window what the blue meant,
The blue circles in the wet square of pasture.

Then at evening the boys drove up the ducks
From the river, squat and uncomplaining,
They herded them here and prisoned them in the
Blue cages. Then they went away. The rain
Sobbed till nightfall in the tamarind trees.

When the rain stopped the ducks began their noise,
Hoarse-throated, full-chested, and we heard them
Away in the big house, after dinner, and my niece
Asked, 'Are they bullfrogs?' I said yes, or perhaps birds.
But I knew all the time they were only ducks.

Their noise is incessant, like frogs or crickets.

And sometimes to me it is like the river
A mile or two away, groaning at its strength.
Or like the rain as it winds the teak groves through.
Or sometimes, to me, like the song of birds.

I am still wondering what they're doing there,
What's being done to them. As I write
Again the rain is washing the still morning small
And the ducks are silent, not at all thinking
What manner of beast creates these hours of sleep.

Snow

Crisp in the winter's morning,
Softly all through the night,
What is this without warning.
     Falling and white?

    I have never seen snow
    But I can imagine it quite—
    Not how it tastes, but I know
         It falls and is white.

One morning I'll open the door
To bring in the morning's milk,
And all around there'll be snow—
     Fallen and still.

How I'll roll in the stuff!
How I'll tumble and spin!
Until the neighbours cry, Enough!
     And send me back in.

The Door

She shut the door because upon the other side
There was the voice of one for whom she once had
      cared:
      She shut the door.

'Open!' he cried, 'for there are things that I must say
'Which you must hear—which will mean much to both
      of us—
      'Open!' he cried.

Remembering how he had marched in thus before,
She turned away and stopped her ears to all his words.
      Remembering.

'When I asked you whether one day you'd shut me out,'
He said with bitterness, 'You replied with a kiss
      'When I asked you!'

She wondered why the words we say to those we want
Sometimes resound in worlds where we have never
      lived
      —She wondered why.

'You must have faith,' he said, 'although to you our
      love
'Appears to limp; with you I'm strong, you're strong
      with me
      '—You must have faith!'

She opened all her mind to all that she had lived,
She summoned all the strength she'd had and turned
      the key,
      She opened all.

He'd never been a man to whom her strength was new;

He'd never thought her precious all was hope enough;
      He'd never been.

These Were My Homes

These were my homes then, though I did not know:
The swell of the womb, and a mother's long breast
And the small peace of a children's house;
The blankets of my bed, and the night's rest
Beneath, and then the waking to sweet air.

These were my homes, though they did not know me
The worn cool green of my father's lands,
Older than battle; the wars that won them;
The moments lingering, for each was planned
And I only had to reach out to sweet air.

Then these are the homes that I will know yet:
One book to live in, one honest page,
One face to meet at dawn and noon and night,
One storm to soothe, one oblivion, one stage,
One bed in which to breathe my last of air.

At last, the homes made on other roads:
But were these mine to know, mine to be told,
I should not tell lest they should become mine.

Integument

Hold me tight, my skin, I fear you may burst
Before your time with ripeness and show the world
My red heart of anger. Hold me tight, I pray
That I may not be compelled to face the worst
with worser still. What, will this blood be shed

From mere longing, saying what cannot be said?

Yet burst if you will, for well I know,
Inside, that inside is another wall
Which will hold off anything that may call
For your destruction. The shield's blazon show
Like a mirror, the vitals of compassion.
It can never burst in such a fashion.
A second skin is something more than skin.

My Father's Hand

My father was such a superman,
He made look easy such difficult things,
It is no easy task to beat a child, yet,
He could do it.
     When his hand landed on my cheek
It made a sound like doom that tore my ears,
I thought my heart would burst.
How will I forget
The tears, the shame? My eyes sting again,
Feeling, remembering.
     What love and caring
We carry each of us and mean to share
Always tomorrow, or in a better world
More wisely made than this, tomorrow
Or perhaps yesterday; what words we have
To soothe hurts, what all, what all to give
And when we give it is with empty hand.

My Mother Would Not

My mother would not kiss or curse
After we reached a certain age:
She was there like India asking
Nothing but faith.
        Now she is grey
I wonder where that mother is
Who I thought knew me complete
But knows only how easily
From my face the lies I tell
And never searches to know more.

Where is she gone My memories say
This is the same mother who held
That all I could say was true.

The secret in the mother's breast
Is what only a child might know
Who without kiss or caress
Prepares to show its face above.

Some secret within India is
No one has found or searches for
Which will not kiss which will not curse
And hangs from itself such a lie
I never will know completely.

Double Bill

Ducks have, in water– but only clear water
And in good light– a kind of double life.
The webs vanish, and they are doubly there
Upside down, beaks and duck's eyes.
                      Only they
When they look down can see both halves,

The webbed and the unwebbed.
                                        A duck
Maybe thinks she has reason to hide
What she does with her feet. She must float
For no one must know she can walk on water.

L' après -midi d'un Canard

Ducks have, in water, a visible class
And grace they completely lack on land.
Do they feel it, to be hypocrites,
To shrug off the clumsy Quasimodo walk
And slip noiselessly into Nijinsky?

Well, hardly Nijinsky: but how easily
They lure the viewer into hyperbole
Just by stepping off, as if they did not know
That turbid, weed-choked pond contained
All they had forgotten of their fate.

Familial: One Gift My Father Gave Me

One gift my father gave me: That was anger,
A stirring in the blood. Between the ears
A drum. Smoke filled my eyes. I scented
Tears and the blood of ancestral ghosts,
Preserved in the teak beams of my father's house.

Another gift he gave, and that was love
Of words. How they come together, make
A song. I can only sing for love. I am
Speechless with song, the sirens never made
Such music as I have heard
Within my head.

Let me now, O muse, marry these two gifts
My father gave, let me unrepentant
Burden my words with anger they cannot bear.

The Rain is Pouring down Again

The rain is pouring down again, and all
The grass is overjoyed. Naturally it knows
Nothing of the jaws that clomp in half
Its pride, the guileful steel that cuts
In two its prime. Why should it grow
Thinking these thoughts? Its seeds scatter
Where its murderers will, and in small days
To come, will sprout again.
                            We who keep our heads
And stunt our hopes, we also know something
That grass has glimmerings of: Of suns gone
Without goodbyes, of parched earth and wayward winds
Which do not wait.
                            And yet our proud roots clutch
At tenuous soil, that holds our lives together
And is willing to be divided at a touch.

GOPIKRISHNAN KOTTOOR

Gopikrishnan Kottoor is an award-winning poet. Apart from his major prizes for poetry such as the All India Poetry Prize (Poetry Society, India) and the All India Special Jury prize (Poetry Society, India and The British Council) he has also won several other prizes and nominations for his poetry. His poems have appeared in magazines of repute both in India and abroad such as *The Illustrated Weekly of India, Opinion, Debonair, Kavya Bharati, Chandrabhaga, Economic and Political Times, The Hindu, Thought, Quest, Chandrabhaga, Kavya Bharati, Indian Literature, Nth position, UK, Orbis, UK, Mud season review, USA, Southwest quarterly USA, Toronto Review, Arabesques, Plaza, Japan, Chiaroscuro, UK*, and others.

His poetry has been translated and published in German, Hindi, and Chinese.

His poetry has featured in anthologies such as Verse, Seattle, India Chapter, Bloodaxe book of Contemporary Indian Poetry in English, The Golden Jubilee Anthology of Indian Poetry in English, Shakespeare Sonnets Global, The Lie of the Land (Sahitya Akademi), 19 Poets, and several others.

Gopikrishnan Kottoor was India Guest at the University of Vienna, Austria, and ICCR nominee for the Foreign Poets Seminar in Tagore Centre, Berlin, Germany.

His major poetry titles include the highly regarded poem sequence on his father, *Father, Wake us in Passing, Mother Sonata, Milestones to the Sun, A Buchenwald Diary, Victoria Terminus, Tell Me, Neruda, The Painter of Evenings, My Blue Alzheimer's Sky, Descent, Vrindavan, The Coloured Yolk of Love (Radha-Krishna poems), Father Benedict Goes to Heaven, Reflections in Silhouette, My dear Tsunami*, and others.

His novels are *A Bridge Over Karma, Chilanka (The anklet), Hill House, Wander (A child's fantasy)*, and *Presumed Guilty* on the life and loves of the fashion designer Anand John.

His dramatic works include *The Mask of Death* (The final Days of John Keats), *Fire in the Soul* (The life of the Nationalist poet Subramania Bharati) *A woman in Flames* and *The Nectar of the Gods*, (The life and execution of the Beatified Devasahayam, a soldier in the army of King Marthanda Varma, Tiruvitamkur).

Gopi Kottoor made his debut in Malayalam with *Yesumuthu, 'Jesus Pearl'* the transcreation of his *Nectar of the Gods* to much critical acclaim.

He has translated Kukoka's *Rati Rahasya* and *Poontanam*.

He edited *A New Book of Indian Poems in English* and *The Mathrubhumi Literary Festival—Poetry Chain* book of poetry readings.

Gopikrishnan Kottoor has been a poetry reviewer for The Hindu Literary Supplement. His poetry reviews and articles have been featured in Malayalam Manorama Online (Guest writer), Deccan Herald, Deccan Chronicle, The Hindu, New English Quarterly, UK, I mantra, Kavya Bharati and The Economic and Political weekly.

Gopikrishnan Kottoor founded Poetry Chain which, with Dr. Paniker as a mentoring spirit was one of the earliest poetry associations for English poetry from Trivandrum, Kerala. Its journal, with a pan Indian spectrum had an uninterrupted run for twenty years from 1997. Poetry Chain published and brought to light many of the poets now in mainstream Indian English Poetry. It worked in association with Poetry Society, India, and on its own, to discover new talent, with awards and poetry promotion such as The Poetry Chain-Poetry Society, (India) awards, The Father, Wake us in Passing Poetry Prize, the Agha Shahid Ali poetry Prize, The Young Talent School Poetry Awards and the Harish Govind Memorial Prize for Poetry.

Gopikrishnan Kottoor is presently working on a compilation of poems, a three-volume collection of poems over the years, a novel, a project based on the life and times of the ever-green celluloid hero Prem Nazir and a rendering into English of the celebrated Malayalam pastoral *Ramanan* by Changampuzha.

Gopikrishnan Kottoor lives in Trivandrum Kerala. Contact him at *gopikottoor@gmail.com*

Printed in Great Britain
by Amazon